CW00348075

REDOUTÉ'S ROSES

Rosa Pomponia Burgundiaca.   *Le Pompon de Bourgogne.*

P. J. Redouté pinx.   Imprimerie de Rémond   Langlois sculp.

P.J. Redouté

REDOUTÉ'S ROSES

Wordsworth Editions

in association with the Natural History Museum, London.

Acknowledgements

The Publishers would like to thank the many people at the Natural History Museum, London, who made publication of this work possible, and in particular R.E.R. Banks, Head of Library Services, Clive Reynard, Head of Publications, Christine Ellwood and her staff in the Botany Library, and Tim Parmenter and his staff in the Photographic Department.

This edition published 1998 by Wordsworth Editions Ltd.
Cumberland House, Crib Street, Ware, Hertfordshire SG12 9ET.

Copyright © Wordsworth Editions Ltd 1990.

All rights reserved. This publication may not be
reproduced, stored in a retrieval system,
or transmitted, in any form or by any means, electronic,
mechanical, photocopying, recording or otherwise,
without the prior permission of the publishers.

Wordsworth® is the registered trademark
of Wordsworth Editions Ltd.

ISBN 1-85326-498-9

Printed and bound in Spain by Gráficas Estella, S.A.

Introduction

PIERRE-JOSEPH REDOUTÉ was born at St-Hubert near Bastogne in what is now Belgium on 10th July 1759, one of three brothers, all of whom had artistic abilities and inclinations. The eldest, Antoine Ferdinand, painted stage sets and theatre decor, and helped with the decoration of the Elysée Palace; Henry Joseph, the youngest, was engaged by Napoleon as an official artist for the Egyptian campaign. Pierre-Joseph himself intended to make his career in religious art, but during his apprenticeship, working in churches in northern Europe painting frescoes and other decorations, he became entranced by the flower paintings of the Dutch School, particularly those of Van Huysum. Although straightened circumstances forced him to join Antoine's studio in Paris for several years, he managed during this time to indulge his taste for flower painting, and some of his small water-colours attracted the attention of two of the greatest botanical artists of the day, Van Spaedonck and Charles Louis L'Heretier.

In 1787, L'Heretier persuaded Redouté to join him in London to help illustrate his great work *Sertum Anglicum* ('An English Garland'). By all accounts, Redouté and his young wife (they had married the previous year) enjoyed their time in London, and Redouté had the opportunity to meet some of the great botanists of the day. Perhaps more important were his meetings with London engravers of Bartolozzi's school and artists such as James Sowerby, from whom Redouté learnt techniques that were to stand him in good stead.

On his return to Paris, he was honoured by being appointed personal art-teacher to Queen Marie-Antoinette, and master draughtsman to her court. This was only the first of several prestigious posts, and Redouté was so apolitical that he became teacher to both wives of Napoleon, the Empresses Josephine and Marie-Louise, and after the restoration of the monarchy in France, to the Duchesse de Berry, Queen Marie-Amelie and to Madame Adelaide. In 1822 he succeeded Van Spaedonck as Professor of Plant Iconography at the Royal Gardens. It was at the time of the restoration that Redouté embarked on publication of his two greatest books, *Les Liliacées* and *Les Roses*.

Les Roses was published in 30 fascicles from March 1817 until March 1824, each generally containing six plates, and each with a commentary by Claude-Antoine Thory. There were two different presentations and impressions: one was an edition of 100 copies, large folio, costing 50 francs per fascicle, and the other, large quarto, sold at 25 francs. The book became the wonder of the age, and it is to be deeply regretted that the original paintings were lost when a fire destroyed the Library of the Louvre. Although their production and publication was primarily for the purposes of scientific accuracy and classification, as Thory's original outline of the work made clear, even there Thory allowed, among all the talk of 'painstaking research' as to varieties, species, 'special characteristics' and so on, that the roses were also selected 'for their beauty'. And it is for the way he captured this beauty that Redouté's magnificent work is now so highly prized.

Redouté went on to publish several other books, including two more on roses, but only one, generally known as *les Plus Belles Fleurs et Fruits* (1827-1833) came near to emulating the magnificence of *Les Roses*. He remained active for the remainder of his life, and died of a stroke aged 81, during the course, appropriately, of a lecture that he was giving at the Jardin des Plantes.

ROSA CENTIFOLIA
'CABBAGE ROSE' (Lit. 'HUNDRED-PETALLED ROSE')

Shrub 1.8–2.1 m high; *branches* with numerous almost straight unequal *prickles*. *Leaflets* 5(–7), deeply bidentate, dark green, underside pubescent; margins and petiole glandular hairy, the latter unarmed. *Receptacles* thick, ovoid, strongly bristly like the pedicels; *sepals* concave, 3 pinnatifid and leaflike, 2 simple, glandular on the outside, downy within; *corolla* rounded, of numerous pink *petals* becoming darker towards the centre of the flower.

Up to the present no native home was known for this rose, but in 1816 Rau stated that it is native to Northern Persia. Roessig claims that the Dog Rose (*Rosa canina*) is the prototype of *R. centifolia* perfected by cultivation over many centuries. If this were so, the specimen with single flowers raised from seed in Dupont's nursery would be its predecessor. Many cultivars are known: Miss Lawrence figured 19, and the Dutch catalogues list over 100, but only the best will be considered here.

To obtain the maximum number of fine blooms, prune the bush in February to keep it dwarf.

Rosa centifolia.   *Rosier a cent feuilles.*

P.J. Redouté pinx.   Imprimerie de Rémond.   Couten sculp.

ROSA BERBERIFOLIA
'BARBERRY-LEAVED ROSE'

At most 0.6 m high; *branches* spreading, pubescent, slender, with many small whitish somewhat recurved *prickles* most commonly in pairs. *Leaves* simple, very shortly petiolate, alternate, serrate, glaucous green. *Receptacles* bristly with numerous short straight prickles; *sepals* lanceolate, entire, simple, also bristly; *flowers* solitary at the branch tips; *corolla* of 5 canary-yellow *petals*, each with a basal purplish spot.

This rose, distinguished from all others by the simple leaves, has been brought back from Persia, where it is very common, by Michaux Sr. and Olivier. The latter sent it to Cels Sr. who flowered it for the first time in Paris. Up to the present no-one has successfully acclimatised it in France, almost all amateurs having lost their plants, and the few surviving seedlings being weakly and languishing. Budding on *R. spinosissima* has given the greatest hope of success.

Rosa Berberifolia.   *Rosier* a feuilles d'Épine-vinette.

P.J. Redouté pinx.   Imprimerie de Rémond   Chapuy sculp.

ROSA SULFUREA
'SULPHUR ROSE'

1.2–1.8 m high or more; *prickles* numerous, dense, subulate, fine, unequally long, yellowish. *Leaflets* 7, ovate, sometimes rotund, dentate, pale green, subglaucous below; petioles prickly; stipules incised. *Flowers* solitary, scentless, pale yellow, on short glabrous pedicels; *receptacles* globose, a little flattened at the top, glabrous or sometimes glandular hairy; *sepals* semi-pinnatifid.

Said to originate from the Levant. On young stems the blooms generally open badly, especially if pruned too hard: only old stems sheltered from both rain and sun can bear this beautiful rose to perfection. Not all soils and climates suit it: it flowers in France and Germany, but according to Andrews has not yet flowered in gardens in and around London.

Rosa Sulfurea.   *Rosier jaune de souffre.*

P.J.Redouté pinx.   Imprimerie de Rémond.   Langlois sculp.

ROSA RUBRIFOLIA
'RED-LEAVED ROSE'

Reddish, glaucous *bush* 2.4–3 m or more high. Stem *prickles* stout, recurved. *Leaves* 5–7 (–9), oblong-ovate, soft to the touch, serrate, glabrous, glaucous, wine-coloured, particularly below; petiole with yellowish prickles; stipules entire. *Flower* red at first, greenish-white when fully developed, clustered at the branch tips; pedicels short, glabrous, with a lanceolate bract at the base; *receptacles* at first ovoid, subglobose at maturity; *sepals* entire, acute, glandular hairy, longer than petals.

This shrub grows naturally in the Dauphiné, the Vosges, and particularly in moist places in the mountains of Auvergne, where we have seen bushes 3 m in height. It readily and promptly naturalises from seed.

Rosa Rubrifolia.   *Rosier a feuilles rougeâtres.*

P. J. Redouté pinx.   Imprimerie de Remond.   Chapuy sculp.

ROSA MOSCHATA
'MUSK ROSE'

Stems 1.8–2.1 m high, armed with strong, stout, hooked *prickles*; petioles with smaller prickles. *Leaflets* 5–9, oblong, acute, serrate, dark green, glossy, underside tomentose. *Flowers* paniculate, faintly scented, white, on slender glandular-hairy pedicels; *receptacles* oblong ovoid, slightly hairy; *sepals* lanceolate, a little shorter than petals, 2 entire, 3 pinnatifid; *styles* villous, exserted in a small column the height of the stamens.

This rose originates in Barbary. It is tender and requires shelter in winter. It flowers late, holds its foliage for a long time, and resents pruning. Olivier has seen it on trees 9 m high in the gardens of the King of Persia at Isfahan. Musk, the perfumed oil that is subject of so much trade in the Levant, is extracted from this rose by distillation at Tunis. A semi-double cultivar is the commonest in cultivation, but another is fully double.

Rosa moschata.

Rosier musque.

P. J. Redouté pinx.

Imprimerie de Remond.

Chapuy sculp.

ROSA BRACTEATA
'BRACTEATE or MACARTNEY ROSE'

Normally sprawling, but rising to some metres high when the stems are supported. *Branches* slender, villous, covered here and there with slightly hooked prickles which are often paired. *Leaflets* 7–9, ovate, obtuse, dentate, cuneate at the base, glossy, glabrous on both sides. *Flowers* 1 (–2), white, scented; pedicel short, greyish velvety as are the *receptacles* and *sepals*; bracts 7–8, imbricate, concave, fringed, pointed, amplexicaul; *petals* heart-shaped, large, notched, mucronate.

Native of China, whence it was brought by Lord Macartney and flowered for the first time by Cels. It is not as tender as is commonly supposed. It survives the winter in the open air with screening only during extreme cold, although in such circumstances it blooms later. In an orangery it holds its leaves all the year round and flowers in spring.

Rosa Bracteata.

Rosier de Macartney

P.J. Redouté pinx.

Imprimerie de Rémond

Chapuy sculp.

ROSA CENTIFOLIA BULLATA [Thory var. n.]
'BULLATE CABBAGE ROSE'

Leaflets rugose and bullate, often very gross and inrolled beneath; petioles pubescent, sometimes with a few fine recurved prickles. Otherwise exactly as for *R. centifolia* (p. 6).

This beautiful modification of *R. centifolia*, known in gardens as the rose with embossed or blistered foliage, or better as the lettuce-leaved rose, has been propagated by Dupont, whose name, *Rosa bullata*, we have retained. It has many virtues over and above those of the common *centifolia*: the closer, less diverging branches which form a beautiful head when grafted on briar; the singular leaves, so voluminous that the petiole seems to support them with difficulty; the beauty, size, rounded shape and sweet perfume of the flowers. It can only be perpetuated as a graft, and as such it is delicate and short-lived. In our rose garden at Belleville near Paris we have tried to get it on its own roots by layering, but obtained only sparse bushes with inferior blooms.

P. J. Redouté pinx.

Imprimerie de Rémond

Langlois sculp.

Rosa centifolia Bullata.
Rosier à feuilles de Laitue.

ROSA MUSCOSA
'[SINGLE] MOSS ROSE'

Bush 0.6–0.9 m high, covered in numerous, straight, unequal, very sharp *prickles*. *Leaflets* 5, ovate, underside pubescent; unequally dentate and glandular towards the margins; petiole villous, unarmed. *Pedicels, receptacles* and pinnatifid *sepals* covered with long, greenish-brown, glandular, viscous, moss-like outgrowths giving off a sweet and penetrating fragrance. *Petals* 5, clear pink. *Heps* not seen.

The single-flowered moss rose, still very rare in France, came to us from England where it bloomed for the first time in the gardens of the Countess of Wandes at Bayswater in 1807. Some consider it a variety of *R. centifolia* or *provincialis*, but it seems to us a distinct species. It needs a good soil and resents exposure to wet. One specimen on a briar stock in Boursault's garden produces roses with 6–7 petals; from an examination of the stamens we infer that, stimulated by grafting, the moss rose tends to doubling. Many beautiful cultivars have arisen from the moss rose – pink and white, both with double blooms. Andrews figures and describes *R. muscosa variegata* with white and pink striped flowers which we have never seen.

Rosa muscosa.   *Rosier mousseux.*

P. J. Redouté pinx.   Imprimerie de Rémond   Gouten sculp.

ROSA MUSCOSA MULTIPLEX
'DOUBLE MOSS ROSE'

Differs from the single moss rose (p. 20) only by the fully double *flowers*, which are up to 8 cm diameter or more, with many series of *petals*, those at the centre crumpled, inrolled and concealing the projecting, divergent *styles*.

Roessig claims that this rose grows naturally in the Alps, but no naturalist before him ventured to give a habitat. Andrews maintains it as a native of England – but English artists consider many plants as native in the absence of a known habitat. However that may be, the double moss rose is widespread and one of the loveliest decorations of our gardens today by virtue of its flower and its perfume. Culture is the same as for the 'Hundred-petalled Rose', from which it differs only by the "mossy" calyx.

Rosa muscosa multiplex. *Rosier mousseux à fleurs doubles.*

P. J. Redouté pinx.   Imprimerie de Rémond   Langlois sculp.

ROSA CLINOPHYLLA [Thory sp. n.]
'DROOPY-LEAVED ROSE'

Smooth, climbing *shrub* 0.9–1.2 m high; *stems* with a short, compact, whitish silky down and fine, straight, geminate *prickles*, scattered but mainly at the base of the stipules. *Leaves* alternate, declinate; *leaflets* 9–11, elliptic, almost always bidentate, bright green, upperside glossy, underside tomentose; petioles villous, glandular, sometimes with 2–3 small hooked prickles; stipules fringed, with elongated, pointed divisions. *Flowers* 1 (–3) at the branch tips on very short pedicels surrounded by alternate floral leaves and bracts like an involucre; pedicels, *receptacles* and entire, subulate *sepals* downy like the stem and branches; *petals* 5, white, slightly yellow at the base; *styles* free, a little exserted; *stamens* almost as long as the sepals.

Rosa clinophylla derives its name from the Greek κλιγω, to droop, and φυλλον, a leaf. It is easily distinguished from all others by the stance of the leaves and by the involucre which seems to enfold the flower. It is cultivated in Boursault's garden, from which our painting was made. It flowers in July and needs to spend the winter in the conservatory where it retains its leaves. Its native country is unknown.

Rosa Clynophylla.   *Rosier à feuilles penchées.*

P. J. Redouté pinx.   Imprimerie de Rémond   Chapuy sculp.

ROSA LUCIDA
'GLOSSY ROSE'

Dense *bush* 1.5–1.8 m tall; *branches* glabrous; *prickles* straight, geminate, associated with the stipules. *Leaflets* 7–9, ovate, glabrous, upperside shining, underside paler; unequally dentate; petiole with some very fine prickles. *Flowers* clear pink, slightly scented, medium sized, 3–4 together in a terminal corymb; *receptacles* and pedicels armed with reddish glandular hairs; *sepals* entire, subspatulate, nearly as long as petals. *Heps* depressed globose, red.

Rosa lucida is native to North America and widespread in gardens where a semi-double cultivar is grown. In full sun it blooms in June; in shade only in August and September. It is not fussy, but demands a good soil. The flowers are short-lived, but follow one another in quick succession.

Rosa Lucida.

Rosier Luisant.

P.J. Redouté pinx.

Imprimerie de Remond

Bessin sculp.

ROSA KAMTCHATICA
'KAMCHATKA ROSE'

Bush 0.6–0.9 m high at most; *stems* and *branches* downy and hispid; *prickles* numerous, straight, unequal, acute, whitish, the shortest often glandular. *Leaflets* 7–9 (–11), upperside dark green, underside paler; soft to the touch, obtuse or more often acute ovate, with unequal glandular teeth; petioles downy, prickly; stipules elongated, ciliate, with purplish glands. *Flowers* 1 (–2), terminal, large, fragrant, red tinged violet, on short, reddish, glabrous pedicels; *receptacles* globose and glabrous; *sepals* entire, subulate, more or less as long as the petals, pubescent outside, tomentose within. *Hep* rounded, glabrous, reddish-brown, crowned by the long-persistent calyx.

This native of Kamchatka flowers in France in June and often also in the autumn. It makes a fine effect when grafted on briar, but blooms sparingly unless pruned. No double-flowered cultivar is yet known. Comparison with Cels's Fig. 67 of the same species reveals that in less than 18 years it has undergone changes in length and density of prickles and form of leaflets.

P. J. Redouté pinx.   Imprimerie de Remond   Chapuy sculp.

Rosa Kamtschatica.   *Rosier du Kamtschatka.*

ROSA INDICA [Thory sp. n.]
'CHINA ROSE'

Bush 0.6 m high; *branches* almost always unarmed. *Leaflets* 5, simply dentate, the two lowest smaller than the others, the odd leaflet much larger; petiole with small recurved prickles. *Flowers* solitary at the branch tips, on long glabrous pedicels; *receptacles* smooth and oblong; *sepals* serrulate; *petals* 5, notched, cordate, from the softest pink up to darkest purple.

Described by Linnaeus as *Rosa indica*, this rather rare rose is to be found in the nurseries of Cels and Noisette. It is multiplied from cuttings and requires a light soil and a conservatory in winter, although it can be grown in the open air if carefully covered during great cold.

In this work, all the Bengal and China roses, cultivated so freely in France and England, are included under the title 'Rosiers des Indes' [China Roses]: the Semperflorens, Chinensis, Longifolia, Indica, Bengalensis and Diversifolia of Ventenat, Persoon, Willdenow and others. They are easily recognised by:–

1. Almost continuous blooming from the start of spring up to the frosts.
2. The two lowest leaflets being always smaller than the others, and the odd one generally much larger.
3. The long filiform stamens which twist after expansion to overhang the filiform, tortuous styles.

Rosa Indica.   *Rosier des Indes.*

P. J. Redouté pinx.   Imprimerie de Rémond.   Chapuy sculp.

ROSA INDICA VULGARIS [Thory var. n.]
'COMMON CHINA ROSE'

Stems smooth, green, 1.2–1.8 m high, with strong, recurved reddish *prickles*. *Leaflets* 3–5, green, glossy, glabrous, simply dentate; petioles ciliate, with small hooked prickles. *Flowers* semidouble, soft pink, faintly scented at the moment of opening, 1 to many, subpaniculate; *receptacles* ovoid; *sepals* almost always pinnate, lightly hispid as are the pedicels.

Popular all over Europe, from palaces to cottage gardens – the most widespread shrub of the genus. The 'Common China' was introduced by the English from India and flowered for the first time in Parson's garden at Rickmansworth, Herts., around 1793. It is known in London nurseries as the 'Pale China Rose'. It is very easily propagated from cuttings, which, if taken in February, often flower the same year. Long treated as tender, it is today grown outdoors where it has withstood the most rigorous winters.

Rosa Indica vulgaris.   *Rosier des Indes commun.*

P. J. Redouté pinx.   Imprimerie de Rémond   Bessin sculp.

ROSA INDICA ACUMINATA [Thory var. n.]
'SHARP-PETALLED CHINA ROSE'

Small *shrub* about 0.6 m tall; *stems* diffuse, glabrous, with sparse, almost straight *prickles* towards the base. *Leaflets* 3–5, acute ovate, bidentate, upperside green, underside paler; flushed purplish. *Flowers* slightly scented, solitary at the branch tips; *receptacles* rounded; pedicels glabrous; *sepals* entire or more often pinnate; *petals* 5, always acuminate, white faintly flushed with pink; *stamens* long, filiform, twisted, bent over the *styles* as in all China Roses.

This should not be confused with Curtis's *Rosa semperflorens minima* which resembles it in the pointed shape and colour of the petals and the purplish flush on the leaflets, but differs in its elongated ovoid receptacle, apparent overall glands and hairs and numerous prickles.

The constantly acuminate petals distinguish this cultivar from its allies where at most the petals are partially or occasionally acuminate. It is almost always in bloom, and requires a conservatory in winter.

Rosa Indica acuminata.   *Rosier des Indes à petales pointus.*

P. J. Redouté pinx.   Imprimerie de Remond   Chapuy sculp.

ROSA MONTEZUMAE [Humboldt sp. n.]
'MONTEZUMA ROSE'

Shrub in habit and height like our dog rose; *branches* cylindrical, smooth, glabrous, unarmed. *Leaflets* 5, ovate, acute, rounded at the base, dentate, up to 25 mm long, glabrou son both surfaces, upperside dark green, underside paler with prominent veins; petioles hairy within, with small, sparse, slightly recurved prickles below; petiolules very short; stipules fringed with very small red glands. *Flowers* solitary at the tips of young branches, the same size as in the dog rose, very sweetly scented; pedicels short, without hair or prickles; *receptacles* ellipsoidal, quite glabrous and unarmed; *sepals* ovate, concave, mucronate, mostly pinnatifid, pubescent and flushed red outside; *petals* clear pink or sometimes almost white, obovate and slightly notched. Ripe *heps* not seen.

Humboldt has been kind enough to send us this rose which he and Bonpland discovered in porphyritic mountains bordering the valley of Mexico in the North, and he has provided a description and observations also. It grows at 3000 m mainly at the summit of Cerro-Ventoso.

Rosa Montezuma   *Rosier de Montezuma*

P.J. Redouté pinx.   Imprimerie de Rémond.   Langlois sculp.

ROSA ALPINA PENDULINA
'PENDENT-FRUITED ALPINE ROSE'

Stems 0.9–1.2 m high, diffuse, quite unarmed as in almost all alpine roses. *Leaflets* 7–9, ovate, obtuse, upperside bright green, underside paler; biserrate; petioles a little rough to the touch, with moderately large finely toothed stipules which widen upwardly. *Flowers* 1 (–2), inclined, sometimes re-erecting; pedicels glandular hispid; *receptacles* oblong, sometimes rounded, distended, glabrous, recurved at anthesis; *sepals* entire, greenish or purplish externally, downy within and on the margins; *petals* 5, emarginate, rose violet; *stamens* numerous; *styles* very short but distinct. Found in mountainous places in Europe and, according to Aiton, indigenous to North America.

Like all the alpine roses, this is very variable. Heps may be much elongated or subglobose, constricted above like a calabash or not at all constricted, sometimes on the same root. The always inclined hep, glandular hispid peduncles and absence of prickles are the only characters for sure recognition. It produces a fine show of its odd pendulous red heps in our gardens in autumn, and is the first of all to bloom in Paris when favourably sited. It demands little attention and all soils seem to suit it.

Rosa Alpina pendulina.

Rosier des Alpes à fruits pendants.

P.J. Redouté pinx.

Imprimerie de Rémond

Bessin sculp.

ROSA ALPINA LAEVIS [Thory var. n.]
Lit. "ALPINE ROSE WITH GLOBOSE RECEPTACLE
AND GLABROUS PEDICEL"

Shrub 1.2–1.5 m high; *stems* elongated, reddish in old age as in the cinnamon rose, quite unarmed. *Leaflets* 5–9, ovate, glabrous, almost always bidentate; petioles slightly hispid; stipules large, denticulate. *Flowers* 1–3, terminal and axillary; pedicels glabrous; bracts ovate, slightly dentate; *receptacles* globose; *sepals* entire, linear, spatulate above, woolly margined; *petals* 5, emarginate, lively red, whitening towards the base; *stamens* very numerous; *styles* distinct.

This native of the Alps and Southern France is often confused with *Rosa cinnamomea* on account of the globose receptacle and stem colour, but the latter has prickles adjacent to the stipules and elongated, always simply dentate leaflets. It flowers in cultivation through the greater part of the summer, and suckers freely.

Rosa Alpina Laevis. *Rosier des Alpes a pedoncule et calice glabres.*

P. J. Redouté pinx.   Imprimerie de Remond   Bessin sculp.

ROSA INDICA FRAGRANS [Thory var. n.]
'TEA-SCENTED CHINA'
(Lit. "SCENTED ROSE OF INDIA")

Stems 0.3–0.4(–0.6) m tall, with sparse, reddish, almost straight *prickles. Leaflets* 3–5, ovate, acute, glabrous, denticulate, underside a little purplish; petiole with small recurved prickles. *Flowers* 7 cm or more in diameter, inclined; pedicels slightly hispid; *petals* flesh-white, as if transparent, in many series, irregularly notched above; *receptacles* globose and *sepals* almost always entire, both glabrous.

This is remarkable among the many China roses by the size and transparency of the petals and the perfume, especially at the time of anthesis. Introduced from the East Indies to England in 1809, it flowered for the first time in the nursery of Colville who distributed it under the imprecise name of tea-scented rose. It passes the winter in the conservatory and is easily propagated by cuttings or, better, budded on the common China. It is often attacked by mildew, caused by cold wet weather in spring. This can be cured by rubbing all the affected parts with a sponge soaked in vinegar, according to Boursault. Perhaps rust and all similar rose ailments could be cured in this way.

Rosa Indica fragrans. *Rosier des Indes odorant.*

(vulg. Bengale à odeur de thé.)

P. J. Redouté pinx.   Imprimerie de Rémond   Langlois sculp.

ROSA DAMASCENA SUBALBA
'BLUSH DAMASK ROSE'

Tufted *bush* 0.9–1.2 m tall; *prickles* unequal, some straight, some recurved, reddish. *Leaflets* 5, simply dentate, upperside glabrous, underside pubescent and sometimes purplish; petiole villous, glandular, with some recurved prickles. *Flowers* 2–3, subpaniculate at the branch tips; pedicels glandular hispid; bracts recurved, acute; *receptacles* distended midway and *sepals* elongated, pointed, pinnatifid, both hairy; *petals* 5, notched, white flushed with pink; bud darkish red.

Many have confused *Rosa damascena* with *R. bifera*. Some have placed it in the centifolia series, and Poiret among the albas. The differences are set out below:–

R. damascena: receptacle swollen towards the middle and narrowing towards both ends.

R. bifera: receptacle funnel-shaped, confluent with the pedicel.

R. alba: receptacle ovoid, globose at the base, like an inverted thimble.

R. centifolia: receptacle ovoid, globose at the top; pedicel much longer; petiolar prickles absent.

This elegant bush produces a large quantity of charming flowers successively for more than a month. It grows in Southern Europe and is thought to be a native of Spain. For a long time rare in gardens and confined to a few nurseries, today amateurs hasten to obtain it now that single-flowered roses are no longer disdained.

Rosa Damascena, subalba. *Rosier de Damas à Pétale teinté de rose.*

P. J. Redouté pinx. Imprimerie de Rémond. Chapuy sculp.

ROSA POMPONIA [Thory sp. n.]
'POMPON ROSE'

Low, branched *bush*; *prickles* sparse, slender, almost straight. *Leaflets* (3–)5, ovate, rugose, clear green, underside tomentose; simply dentate, a little ciliate, margins glandular; petioles villous. *Flowers* fully double, sweetly scented, mostly in pairs at the branchlet tips; pedicels, *receptacles* and the pinnatifid *sepals* hispid from black, stalked, slightly sticky glands; *petals* very many, pink deepening towards the centre of the bloom.

This is probably a cultivar derived from either *R. centifolia* or the Provence rose, with which it has great similarity. Many further derivatives are known with white, striped or almost single flowers, plus others with blooms of various sizes whose identity with this group is not proven.

To encourage new spring growth one should prune hard after flowering as the stems and principal branches die back. Propagation is by division of the old rootstocks in autumn.

Rosa Pomponia.

Rosier Pompon.

P. J. Redouté pinx.

Imprimerie de Rémond

Langlois sculp.

ROSA VILLOSA
'SHAGGY ROSE'

Stems to more than 3.6 m tall; *prickles* sparse, almost straight, greyish. *Leaflets* 5 or 7, bidentate, soft to the touch, woolly on both sides; petiole tomentose, often with small, very short prickles. *Flowers* faintly scented, 2–3 together at the branch tips; pedicels and *receptacles* glandular hispid; *sepals* a little pinnatifid, pubescent, glandular, with an elongated, often flattened, leaflike tip; *petals* 5, cordately notched, clear red in cultivated plants but sometimes off-white in the wild.

Rosa villosa grows in Europe in hills, hedges and thickets. It is somewhat changed by cultivation, as can be seen from our plate which is taken from a long-cultivated individual. It is easily distinguished by the numerous soft appressed greyish hairs covering the leaflets, and the very large bristly heps, giving the name 'Apple Rose'. Two varieties which have been raised to specific rank by many authors are *R. mollissima* Willd., differing only by its glabrous receptacle, and *R. tomentosa* Smith, which has an ovoid receptacle and simply dentate leaflets. Desvaux has made *R. tomentosa* a variety of *R. canina*, and Rau makes a new variety *R. villosa minuta* which differs only in the subovoid receptacle, more elongated leaflets and heps smaller by a half.

In some countries the heps are dried and eaten in winter like prunes, or are made into an agreeable conserve. Trouble-free to grow, *R. villosa* prefers shade to full sun. Semi-double and double cultivars are also in cultivation.

Rosa Villosa, Pomifera.   *Rosier Velu, Pomifere.*

P.J. Redouté pinx.   Imprimerie de Remond.   Chapuy sculp.

ROSA EGLANTERIA
'AUSTRIAN BRIAR' (Lit.'[YELLOW] WILD BRIAR')

Stem often over 3.6 m tall; *branches* and branchlets numerous, spreading, slender, greenish-brown; *prickles* straight, distant. *Leaflets* 5 or 7, ovate, obtuse, deeply bidentate, glandular, somewhat shining and sticky, upperside dark green, underside paler; petioles rough to the touch, more or less armed with small prickles. *Flowers* 1–3 at the branch tips on glabrous pedicels; *receptacles* globose, glabrous; *sepals* subulate, entire or pinnatifid; *corolla* to 7 cm diameter; *petals* 5, of a beautiful pale yellow; *styles* in a globose head, with more or less dark purple stigmas.

This is easily recognised by the foetid scent of the flowers but pleasantly fragrant leaves which smell like apples when bruised. It is undemanding in culture and left to itself attains a great height and could cover an arbour, but it resents pruning. It should not be confused with the dog rose or sweetbriar which are also referred to as 'Eglantier' by many authors.

It grows in England, Germany and in Southern France; several authors consider it native to the Paris area. We have never seen the double-flowered cultivar, but it is claimed to occur in gardens in the valley of Montmorency. Perhaps it has been confused with *Rosa sulfurea* which is very different. Vilmorin has obtained from seed an attractive dwarf cultivar.

Rosa Eglanteria

Rosier Eglantier.

P. J. Redouté pinx.

Imprimerie de Rémond.

Langlois sculp.

ROSA EGLANTERIA PUNICEA
'AUSTRIAN COPPER' (Lit. 'CORN POPPY ROSE')

The Nasturtium, Countess or Austrian Rose of gardens differs from the preceding only in:

1. *Petals* of a fine ochreous within, yellow-orange outside, sometimes striped yellow or purplish ('Tulip Rose' of Du Pont);

2. *Stems* and *branches* flushed red, whereas the yellow briar has them greenish-grey;

3. *Flowers* less foetid, and *leaves* less fragrant.

In spite of these differences, most naturalists consider both roses to be one and the same species, for the simple reason that both may occur on one stem. Haller, Leysser and other authors have united *R. eglanteria* and *R. rubiginosa* on account of their almost identically scented leaves, but the colour and small size of the blooms of *rubiginosa*, as well as their distinctive odour, and the very variable form of the receptacle compared with the constantly globose form in *eglanteria* serve to keep the two species apart.

R. eglanteria punicea suckers freely and is adaptable to all soils.

Rosa Eglanteria var. punicea.   *Rosier Eglantier var. couleur ponceau.*

P.J. Redouté pinx.   Imprimerie de Rémond.   Coutan sculp.

ROSA GALLICA OFFICINALIS
'COMMON PROVINS ROSE'

Bush about 0.9 m high; *prickles* weak, sparse, unequal, almost straight. *Leaflets* acute ovate, denticulate; petioles hispid, glandular, with small hooked prickles; stipules acute, denticulate, glandular. *Flowers* semi-double, notable for their size and fine purplish-red *petals;* pedicels 1–2 together at the branch tips, hispid; *receptacles* ovoid, glandular hairy at the base; *sepals* 3 pinnatifid and 2 entire.

Although a native of Southern France, this rose seems to dislike too warm a site in our gardens. The soil in which it is grown affects the size of the blooms. This is the rose grown principally for use in pharmacy – from it is made syrup and conserve.

No species of rose has produced more numerous descendants than the French or Provins Rose, this group alone comprising almost a half of all cultivated roses. Dutch catalogues list many hundreds, but differences which the eye can see the language of botany is inadequate to express. We therefore cite only the most remarkable and those generally in cultivation, especially if already figured or described. Under *gallica* we include, as can be seen, many species which have been separated, because experience and more than twenty years of cultivation show us that these are only trifling variants.

Rosa Gallica officinalis.

Rosier de Provins ordinaire.

P.J. Redouté pinx.

Imprimerie de Rémond.

Langlois sculp.

ROSA CENTIFOLIA FLORE SIMPLICI
'SINGLE-FLOWERED CABBAGE ROSE'

Similar to the hundred-petalled rose (p. 6) except for having 5 *petals* only, *stems* less prickly and pedicels and *sepals* with fewer glands. The plate is made from the plant in Noisette's nursery, probably the only one in France now, having come to him after the dispersal of Du Pont's collection, where it was raised from seed.

The two editions of Aiton greatly confuse cultivars of the hundred-petalled and Provins roses, suggesting that the author had not sufficiently observed the two groups. *Rosa centifolia* differs from *R. gallica* by:

1. *Leaflets* soft to the touch, more or less pendent, always gland-edged, rather deeply dentate (those of *gallica* being firm, as if brittle, finely dentate, more or less whitish below and rarely gland-edged).

2. Petioles hispid but always without prickles (those of *gallica* being more or less armed).

An amateur with a little experience can distinguish the two species at a glance.

Rosa Centifolia simplex.   *Rosier Centfeuilles à fleurs simples.*

P. J. Redouté pinx.   Imprimerie de Rémond   Chapuy sculp.

ROSA CENTIFOLIA CARNEA
'VILMORIN ROSE'

Bush on its own roots about 0.6 m tall; *stems* more or less bristly with *prickles* and stiff glandular hairs according to age and the climate in which it grows. *Leaflets* clear green, underside tomentose; petiole glandular, rough to the touch. *Flowers* medium-sized, almost fully double, (1–)2–3 at the branch tips, fragrant, finally of a very pleasant flesh colour distinct from the common *centifolia*, but similar to that of *R. bifera carnea* which is distinguished by the receptacle shape and the almost round, simply dentate leaflets.

This fine rose commemorates Vilmorin, who had a complete collection of roses long before Du Pont, and introduced and propagated it some 15 or 16 years ago. It is very prone to colour mutation, especially when vigorous, so that on a single root one finds flesh-coloured, pink and parti-coloured blooms. It can also transform wholly into a plant with flowers like common *centifolia* but slightly smaller, in which state some nurserymen offer it as 'Pink Vilmorin Rose'.

It needs to be renewed by grafting since it inevitably becomes lost if left to itself, and layers establish with difficulty.

Rosa Centifolia carnea.　　　　　*Rosier Vilmorin.*

P. J. Redouté pinx.　　　　Imprimerie de Rémond.　　　　Charlin sculp.

ROSA CAROLINA CORYMBOSA
'CORYMBOSE CAROLINA ROSE'

Shrub 1.5–1.8 m high; *branches* smooth, reddish, with sparse, unequal, almost straight *prickles*, especially at the base. *Leaflets* 5 or 7, oblong-ovate, opaque, upperside green, underside paler; simply denticulate; petioles pubescent, with short, sharp hooked prickles; two slightly curved yellowish prickles at the base of each young branch. *Flowers* faintly scented, terminal, 3-6 in a short, compact corymb; pedicels more or less hispid; peduncles quite glabrous; bracts ovate, pointed, 2 per pedicel; leafy bracts at the base of the peduncle; *receptacles* globose, bare or more often hispid; *sepals* entire, elongated, spatulate, acute, downy within and on the margins, glandular hispid outside; *petals* 5, clear pink, cordately notched and sometimes mucronate; *stamens* very numerous; stigmas pink, in a convex head.

This is only a variety of *R. caroliniana* Michx., wrongly made into a species by Willdenow. That differs in being only 0.5–0.6 m tall, and having acute, coriaceous, glossy leaflets 25–30 mm long and flowers 1–2 together. The Pennsylvanian Rose has similar corymbs but a constantly glabrous ovary and no petiolar prickles. There is a strong similarity between *Rosa cinnamomea, maialis, carolina, pensylvanica* and *corymbosa* and perhaps they should all be brought together into a single group. This is cultivated in the Jardin des Plantes, Paris, and is notable for the elegance of its habit and the beauty of its corymbs which appear from late July to September.

Rosa Carolina Corymbosa.   *Rosier de Caroline en Corymbe.*

P. J. Redouté pinx.   Imprimerie de Remond   Langlois sculp.

ROSA PIMPINELLIFOLIA MARIAEBURGENSIS
'BURNET ROSE OF MARIENBOURG'

In habitat scarcely 0.5 m high, but o. 9–1.2 m high in cultivation. Stem *prickles* unequal, almost straight, falling with age to leave the *stems* rough as in all this group. New shoots with uniform, somewhat reddish, dense, very sharp *prickles*. *Leaflets* 9 or 11, obtuse ovate, simply dentate but entire at the base; petiole with small, yellow, slightly curved prickles. *Flowers* 5 cm or more in diameter, fragrant, solitary at the ends of the laterals; pedicel and *receptacles* glabrous; *sepals* simple, lanceolate; *petals* 5, white, yellowing towards the base, more or less notched; *stigmas* sessile. *Hep* black and inclined at maturity.

This rose grows in the Alps and in the Ardennes near to the home country of the painter of this work, whose brother Henry Redouté, a member of the Institute of Egypt and natural history painter, discovered it. It requires full sun and almost never blooms in the shade.

Following other authors we have united *Rosa pimpinellifolia* and *R. spinosissima*, which are but varieties of one species having in common simply dentate leaflets and one-flowered peduncles.

Rosa Pimpinelli folia Mariæburgensis.　　　*Rosier de Marienbourg.*

P. J. Redouté pinx.　　　Imprimerie de Rémond　　　Chapuy sculp.

ROSA PIMPINELLIFOLIA PUMILA
'DWARF BURNET ROSE'

Dwarf *shrub* 0.3–0.4 m high, the plate showing a full-length branch cut near the root. *Stems* brown, with many straight, unequal, densely crowded *prickles*. *Leaflets* 7 or 9, elliptical, simply dentate, glabrous as is the petiole; stipules acute. *Flowers* solitary at the tips of the laterals; pedicels and rounded *receptacles* quite glabrous; *sepals* simple, sometimes bifid or slightly denticulate at the tip; *petals* 5, white, yellowing towards the base, cordately notched, concave, the bloom remaining subspherical or cup-shaped almost up to petal fall. *Hep* small, red turning black at maturity.

This is related to *Rosa involuta* Smith by the cup-shaped corolla, but that is distinguished by having hispid pedicels and receptacles. It also approaches De Candolle's *R. myriacantha*, but that has much longer prickles, bidentate leaflets and hispid pedicels.

It is rather rare in gardens, being neglected on account of its small size, but in spring it offers attractive sprays of bloom. In some German towns it is marketed for its early, sweetly fragrant flowers. It grows on mountains in arid places in Northern Europe. A specimen sent to us from near Vienna and cultivated for six years at Belleville still retains its diagnostic characters. It suckers little and forms layers with difficulty, and also dislikes pruning.

Rosa Pimpinelli folia Pumila.　　　　*Petit Rosier Pimprenelle.*

P. J. Redouté pinx.　　　　Imprimerie de Rémond　　　　Chapuy sculp.

ROSA MUSCOSA ALBA
'WHITE MOSS ROSE'

Similar to the 'Double Moss Rose' (p. 22) except that the blooms are white with a very slight pink flush – never absolutely white. Shailer, the English nurseryman, first distributed this beautiful rose four to five years ago. It is presumed to be a hybrid between *Rosa centifolia nivea* and the 'Common Moss'; it certainly offers some of the characters of both. Boursault introduced it to France where it is much propagated although as yet it is not widespread. Andrews lists five varieties of moss rose.

The 'White Moss Rose' needs a sheltered situation and flourishes only in a gritty and somewhat moist soil.

Rosa Muscosa alba　　　　　*Rosier Mousseux a fleurs blanches.*

P.J. Redouté pinx.　　　　　Imprimerie de Rémond.　　　　　Langlois sculp.

ROSA ARVENSIS OVATA
'OVOID-FRUITED FIELD ROSE'

Tortuous, rampant *shrub* appearing upright by supporting itself on trees and bushes; *branches* elongated, reddish and sometimes violet; *prickles* recurved, moderately strong. *Leaflets* 7, ovate, glabrous, upperside green, underside paler; petioles pubescent, prickly. *Flowers* scented, white; pedicels slightly hispid, in a cyme at the tips of the laterals; *receptacles* ovoid, glabrous; *petals* and *stamens* inserted at the edge of a fleshy disc; *styles* aggregated into a short glabrous column, separating above into many distinct *stigmas*.

The key character that separates this group from all others was discovered by La Chenal, who first pointed out the arrangement of styles in *R. arvensis*. De Candolle noted it thereafter in different forms in different individuals and proposed SYNSTYLAE as one of the main subdivisions of the genus. Today the group is divided into 4 sections:–

A	Styles in a long, glabrous column		
		B Sepals almost entire	*R. arvensis*
		BB Sepals elongated, pinnatifid	*R. stylosa*
AA	Styles in hispid column		
		C Stem rampant; peduncle few-flowered	*R. sempervirens*
		CC Stem erect; flowers corymbose	*R. moschata*
AAA	Styles in a very short column		*R. leucochroa brevistyla*

Desvaux and Duhamel have included *Rosa setigera* Michx. here. The sepals, which bear very fine pinnules, seem to accord, but we could not judge the state of the styles from dried specimens.

Rosa arvensis ovata.   *Rosier des champs à fruits ovoïdes.*

P. J. Redouté pinx.   Imprimerie de Rémond.   Chapuy sculp

ROSA BREVISTYLA
Lit. 'SHORT-STYLED ROSE WITH YELLOWISH WHITE FLOWERS'

Tufted *bush* 1.8–2.4 m high; *branches* diffuse, glabrous; *prickles* sparse, broad, hooked and reddish. *Leaflets* 7, upperside green, underside paler; ovate, pointed, simply dentate; petiole with small, yellow, curved, unequal prickles; stipules narrow, pointed, glabrous. *Flowers* 3–4 in a short, dense, terminal corymb, slightly scented, white, yellowing towards the base of the *petals;* peduncles glabrous but pedicels hairy, rough to the touch; bracts 2, ovate, elongated and pointed; *receptacles* subovoid, glabrous; *sepals* pinnatifid, spatulate, slightly villous at the margins; *petals* 5, deeply cordately notched; *styles* coherent into a very short, glabrous column expanded above into many distinct stigmas.

This comes from the Haut-Poitou in Anjou, and three varieties are recognised, var. *systyla* being rarer than the others. All three have been sent us from La Flèche by Le Meunier, and we cultivate them successfully.

Rosa Brevistyla leucochroa.

Rosier à court-style.
(var. à fleurs jaunes et blanches).

P.J. Redouté pinx.   Imprimerie de Rémond   Lemaire sculp.

ROSA RUBIGINOSA TRIFLORA
'THREE-FLOWERED SWEETBRIAR'

1.5–1.8 m high; *prickles* numerous, hooked, unequal. *Leaflets* 5 or 7, rough to the touch, underside and margins covered with sticky, often reddish, glandular hairs, pleasantly wine-scented when bruised. *Flowers* 2–3(–5) at the branch tips; pedicels hispid; *receptacles* ovoid, glabrous; *styles* villous, little exserted; *stigmas* in a convex head.

Rosa rubiginosa is very common in hedgerows and thickets, and is related to the Hedge Rose (*R. sepium*). That differs in having taller stems; more numerous, denser prickles; scentless, elongated, remote leaflets acute at both ends, and by the almost always glabrous, divergent styles.

Rosa Rubiginosa triflora.

Rosier Rouillé à trois fleurs.

P. J. Redouté pinx.

Imprimerie de Rémond

Chapuy sculp.

ROSA HUDSONIANA SALICIFOLIA [Thory sp. et var. n.]
'WILLOW-LEAVED HUDSON ROSE'

Shrub 0.6–0.9 m tall; *stems* glabrous, green, reddish where exposed to sunlight, quite unarmed. *Leaflets* 5 or 7, ovate to oblong, similar to those of the willow *(Salix viminalis)*, upperside green, underside glaucous; simply denticulate; petioles villous, often with 2–3 hooked prickles; stipules elongated, revolute. *Flowers* umbellate or cymose at the branch tips; pedicels frequently glandular, with 2 ovate, pointed, ciliate bracts; *receptacles* generally glabrous, some-times with glandular hairs, especially at the base; *sepals* entire, very long; *petals* 5, of an attractive darkish pink, rounded or often acuminate.

This rose was sent by Du Pont, who confused it with *Rosa carolina*, whereas others have confused it with *R. blanda*. It is near to *R. alpina*, but differs in the simply serrate leaflets, petioles for the most part prickly, conduplicate but not dilated stipules and corymbose flowers. *R. carolina* differs in its stipular prickles; *R. blanda* by its first-year stems bearing straight, subreflexed, narrow prickles and white flowers.

We have dedicated this rose, overlooked until now, to the celebrated English navigator Hudson who discovered the Bay which bears his name and where the rose grows naturally. It is very common in nurseries and comes easily from seed, flowering in the third year. It requires only ordinary care.

Rosa Hudsoniana Salicifolia.

Rosier d'Hudson à feuilles de Saule.

P. J. Redouté pinx.

Imprimerie de Rémond

Langlois sculp.

ROSA ALBA REGALIS
'ROYAL WHITE ROSE'

Shrub 0.6–0.9 m high with smooth, greenish *stems; prickles* sparse, a little curved. *Leaflets* ovate, pubescent, underside pale; petiole villous, prickly. *Flowers* many together at the branch tips; pedicels glandular hispid; *receptacles* ovoid, abruptly rounded at the base, with a few similar bristles; *petals* very large, white flushed pink, in many series. Similar to 'Cuisse de Nymphe' and, because of the larger flowers (7.5 cm upwards), commonly called 'Great Cuisse de Nymphe'. The English call it 'Great Maiden's Blush'. To ensure a succession of fine blooms some of the buds should be sacrificed.

The principal characters distinguishing the White Roses from other series are the ovate, simply dentate leaflets, pubescent below, and the abruptly rounded bases of the receptacles.

Rosa alba Regalis.

Rosier blanc Royal.

P. J. Redouté pinx.   Imprimerie de Remond   Bessin sculp.

ROSA MOSCHATA FLORE SEMI-PLENO
'SEMI-DOUBLE MUSK ROSE'

Differs from the single-flowered *moschata* (p. 14) only by the fewer, weaker *prickles*, *leaflets* tomentose underneath and *corolla* of 3–4 series of petals.

If it is true, as botanists and travellers have told us, that this rose is native to Hindustan, the exquisitely musk-scented blooms are those used along with the Kashmir Rose as the source of the precious essence called Attar by the Indians. This is found floating on the surface of distilled rose water, and is gathered up while still warm with cotton at the end of a stick. The history of its discovery is as curious as it is unique. Langlès in 1804 quotes from a valuable Mogul history: «At a feast given by the Princess Nour-Dyhan for the Emperor Jehangir, a small canal in the gardens was filled with rose water. When the emperor was strolling beside the canal with her, they noticed a kind of foam floating on the surface: the essence of roses concentrated into a mass by the action of the sun. By common consent, this oily substance was pronounced the most delicate perfume known in all India. Subsequently art has striven to imitate what was a product of chance and Nature.»

Rosa moschata forms, with *R. sempervirens*, the third division of the Synstylae.

Rosa Moschata flore semi-pleno   *Rosier* Muscade à fleurs semi-doubles.

P. J. Redouté pinx.   Imprimerie de Remond   Charlin sculp.

ROSA REDUTEA GLAUCA
Lit. 'REDOUTE'S ROSE WITH GLAUCOUS LEAVES'

Bush about 1 m tall; current *branches* with numerous, almost straight, unequal, red *prickles*, those on the old wood persistent and yellowish. *Leaflets* 5 or 7, ovate, acute, glabrous, glaucous green, simply dentate, underside more or less red; petioles with 2–3 small prickles; stipules purplish, quite entire, glandular at the tip. *Flowers* 2–3 together at the tips of the laterals; pedicels hispid, reddish, with ovate pointed bracts below; *receptacles* ovoid to globose, glabrous, flushed red; *petals* 5, white flushed pink and flecked with dark red inside and at the apex, striped with 2–3 reddish longitudinal bands outside; *sepals* entire or rarely with some very fine pinnules, downy within, glandular on the outside, longer than the corolla; *stamens* very numerous; *stigmas* in a sessile head. *Heps* ellipsoidal.

Up to now this has been confused with *R. pimpinellifolia*, but it differs in:–

1. Prickles persisting on adult stems, not deciduous as in *pimpinellifolia*;

2. Peduncles many-flowered, not uniflorous as in *pimpinellifolia*;

3. Sepals longer than the corolla in bud, not shorter as in *pimpinellifolia*.

It should be considered as a hybrid of *R. pimpinellifolia* and *rubrifolia*, and the type of a new rose dedicated to the painter of this work.

Rosa Redutea glauca.

Rosier Redoute a feuilles glauques.

J. Redouté pinx.   Imprimerie de Rémond.   Chapuy sculp.

ROSA REDUTEA RUBESCENS
Lit. 'REDOUTE'S ROSE WITH RED STEMS AND PRICKLES'

Shrub about 0.8 m high; *branches* pliant, elongated, reddish brown, covered in red, unequal, straight, slightly inclined *prickles*. *Leaflets* 7–11, elliptic, some rounded, some pointed, simply dentate, glabrous on both sides, upperside shining; petiole glabrous but sometimes with small hooked prickles. *Flowers* faintly scented, 2–3 together at the tips of the laterals; pedicels, *receptacles* and *calyx* with very short, dense, rather stiff prickles; *sepals* simple, rarely pinnate; *petals* 5, cordately notched, pink, yellowish towards the base. *Heps* subglobose, dark red.

The outstanding feature here is the overall reddish colour during flowering: the leaves begin bright green and shining like box but end the season vivid red. *Rose hispida* Poir. resembles it in having two-flowered peduncles, but has stiff, short, equal bristles rather than prickles, very short sepals and yellowish petals; *R. redutea* is further distinct by its glossy leaflets glabrous on both surfaces, the red prickles and the many-flowered peduncles. It differs from *R. rubrispina* Poir. by having flowers in twos or threes, much longer prickles, globose hips and in its habit.

It came from Du Pont's collection but was apparently lost by the time this was handed over to the government. We grow it in our gardens at Fleury and Belleville, but have not encountered it in any nursery.

Rosa Redutea rubescens.

Rosier Redouté a tiges et a épines rouges.

P. J. Redouté pinx.
Imprimerie de Remond.
Bessin sculp.

ROSA CINNAMOMEA
'MAY ROSE'

Shrub to 3 m or more; *stems* tawny red, pruinose, with paired *prickles* close to the leaf stipules and also to the insertion of young branches which have at their bases other densely clustered, straight, unequal and recurved prickles. *Leaflets* simply dentate, acute at the base, almost always obtuse at the apex, upperside bright green, underside pubescent; petiole villous. *Flowers* semi-double, agreeably scented, 1 (–3); *receptacles* subglobose; *sepals* entire, subspatulate; *petals* reddish, notched, in 3–4 series; *stigmas* in a globose head.

This abundant rose, which grows wild in almost all European countries, has received the name of 'Cinnamon Rose' because of the stem colour, not from the scent of the flowers. It is attractive and in demand because of its early flowering.

Rosa Cinnamomea Maialis.   *Rosier de Mai.*

P. J. Redouté pinx.   Imprimerie de Remond.   Chapuy sculp.

ROSA BIFERA OFFICINALIS
'PERFUMER'S ROSE'

Bush 1.2–1.5 m high; *prickles* rather reddish, unequal, the longest ones recurved. *Leaflets* 3 or 5, ovate, mostly acute, simply dentate, upperside bright green, underside and margins paler and pubescent but without the glandular hairs of *centifolia*; petioles villous, with small hooked prickles at the base and glandular stipules. *Flowers* highly perfumed, scattered, not clustered and erect as in *bifera vulgaris*; *receptacles* bristly with viscous, reddish glandular hairs, passing over into the pedicels which are distinguishable only by having denser, stiffer hairs; *sepals* pinnatifid, elongated, spatulate and often leafy at the tip; *petals* 4–5-seriate, cordately notched, lively pink. This cultivar, known as 'Rosier de Puteaux', is the one normally used in perfumery.

Roses of the *bifera* group are separated from all others by the funnel-shaped receptacle; from *centifolia* they are further removed by having subcorymbose flowers, more recurved prickles and leaflets devoid of glandular hairs on the margins.

Rosa bifera officinalis.　　　　　*Rosier des Parfumeurs.*

P. J. Redouté pinx.　　　　Imprimerie de Rémond.　　　　Langlois sculp.

ROSA DAMASCENA COCCINEA
'PORTLAND ROSE'

Bushy *shrub* 0.4–0.5 m tall; stem *prickles* unequal, closely set, very fine, recurved, scarcely dilated at the base. *Leaflets* 5 or 7, ovate, simply dentate, underside tomentose; petiole villous. *Flowers* 3–4 at the branch tips, subumbellate, faintly scented; pedicels and *receptacles* glandular hispid; *sepals* elongated, spatulate, simple or more often pinnatifid; *petals* 2–3-seriate, cordately notched, of a beautiful purple colour.

The catalogue of *damascena* cultivars ends with *R. damascena variegata* the 'York and Lancaster Rose', having pink, white and parti-coloured blooms from the same root. The name alludes to the warring factions of fifteenth century England where one side chose a red rose as emblem and the other white.

Rosa Damascena Coccinea.

Rosier de Portland.

P. J. Redouté pinx.

Imprimerie de Remond

Bossin sculp.

ROSA CENTIFOLIA MUTABILIS
'UNIQUE ROSE'

Shrub 0.6 m high. *Flowers* 1–4 at the branch tips, rounded, moderately large, a little less double than in common *centifolia; petals* cordately notched, dull velvety white; otherwise like the remainder of the *centifolias*.

This rose, known as 'Rose Unique' or 'Snow-white Rose' was named *R. mutabilis* by Persoon because the bud, bright red at first, opens dull white retaining a reddish hue only in the 5 outermost petals, although the centre petals also retain a pink flush – a throwback to common *centifolia* from which it is derived.

It was discovered by accident about 1777 in a hedge in Suffolk, according to Andrews who gives full details. It flowers a little later than the other *centifolias*. In absence of seeds it can be propagated from cuttings or layers, but is normally grafted on *canina*. However, it succeeds better and has finer blooms if worked on vigorous stocks of the 'Quatre Saisons' rose. It should be pruned hard in February.

Rosa Centifolia mutabilis.   *Rosier unique.*

P. J. Redouté pinx.   Imprimerie de Rémond.   Bessin sculp.

ROSA CENTIFOLIA CARYOPHYLLEA
'CARNATION ROSE'

Slightly tufted *bush* about 0.6 m high; *stems* divergent, green, with fairly numerous *prickles*, some very small, others long, reddish, slightly recurved, especially those near the stipules. *Leaflets* 3–5, acute ovate, upperside bright green, underside paler and to-mentose, margins lightly hirsute, with glandular hairs; petioles villous, often more or less viscous glandular; stipules elongated, acute, incised, villous, glandular. *Flowers* 3(–6), terminal; peduncle with small unequal acicles; pedicels with minute prickles mixed with stiff glandular hairs, the lateral ones bearing acute, oval bracts; *receptacles* ovoid, a little constricted at the top, partially covered in sessile, sticky glands; *sepals* 3 pinnatifid, 2 simple, to-mentose within and similarly glandular on the outside and margins; *corolla* rather small, cup-shaped; *petals* 5–6-seriate, irregularly notched, those at the centre crumpled, a delicate pink streaked with yellowish-white spots; claw elongated, white; *styles* long, villous. *Heps* identical with those of *centifolia*.

This rose, whose flowers resemble a carnation, had a chance origin from a plant of *centifolia* which had degenerated in a garden at Mantes-sur-Seine in 1800. It can be propagated only by budding or layering, and Du Pont preserved and multiplied it under the name of *R. caryophyllata*. It freely reverts to the parent cultivar so to keep it one must renew it by budding on the hedge rose or vigorous shoots of the white rose, which induces magnificent heads and many blooms. It is rarely found on its own roots, and favours a situation facing East.

Rosa Centifolia Caryophyllea.

Rosier Œillet.

P. J. Redouté pinx.

Imprimerie de Rémond.

Charlin sculp.

ROSA INDICA PUMILA
'DWARF CHINA'

Shrub scarcely 20–25 cm high; branching *stems* with sparse, almost straight *prickles* dilated at the base, the lower ones somewhat reddish. *Leaflets* 3 or 5, ovate, upperside dark green, underside paler; rather elongated, glabrous on both sides, finely serrate; petiole with very fine prickles and scarcely visible glandular hairs; stipules incised, with glandular margins. *Flowers* pink, 1 (–3); pedicels long, glabrous or sometimes with minute glandular hairs; *receptacles* ovoid; *sepals* spatulate, often leafy at the tip, almost always pinnatifid; *petals* 4–5-seriate and varying in size according to the time of year, irregularly notched, some pointed.

This dwarf rose flowers uninterruptedly in our gardens from the middle of May up to the autumn frosts. It was introduced by Noisette from Colville who raised it from seed in England a dozen years ago and grew it in his nursery under the name 'Bengale Pompon'. It is easier to propagate from cuttings than any other China rose and can bloom at a height of only 5–8 cm, but with smaller flowers proportional to the size and vigour of the plant. If pruning is neglected the adult branches blacken, the wood dries out and the rose languishes and dies. One should cut it back to within 3 cm of the roots to stimulate new growth and a succession of flowers.

Rosa Indica Pumila.   *Rosier nain du Bengale.*

P. J. Redouté pinx.   Imprimerie de Rémond   Chapuy sculp.

ROSA ALBA FLORE PLENO
'DOUBLE WHITE ROSE'

Diffusely branched *shrub* up to 3–3.6 m high; *branches* smooth, fresh green in youth, with sparse, slightly recurved *prickles;* current shoots almost always glabrous and unarmed. *Leaflets* 5 or 7, rounded, upperside dark green, underside paler and pubescent; petiole villous, with small hooked prickles. *Flowers* 1–4, lateral and terminal; peduncles and pedicels glandular hispid, *receptacles* less so or almost glabrous; *sepals* alternately entire and pinnatifid; *corolla* rarely full, very often semi-double, with the characteristic fragrance of *Rosa alba; petals* white, cordately notched.

Left to itself this rose always tends to throw single flowers and others with only 7–8 petals. The bud is often lightly flushed with pink. It has been figured in many works, but the early plates by Dodonaeus and J. Bauhin are poor.

The Double or Semi-double White Rose flourishes in wild places as in vineyard and garden hedgerows, tolerating shade and demanding little care. By virtue of its height it can make good hedges. Desvaux asserts that the single white *R. alba* has never been seen in the wild. However, Poiret says that it is found in Southern Europe, and Bastard records it from hilly places in the high Poitou, near Angers and Saumur, and finally we have already said that it is to be found in the Rhineland region of Hesse.

The Hill Rose (*R. collina* Jacq.) differs from *R. alba* only by the pink, always simple, subcorymbose flowers, and the hispid-glandular petioles and leaves.

Rosa alba flore pleno.   *Rosier blanc ordinaire.*

P. J. Redouté pinx.   Imprimerie de Remond   Langlois sculp.

ROSA PIMPINELLIFOLIA FLORE RUBRO MULTIPLICI
'DOUBLE RED BURNET ROSE'

This rare and beautiful cultivar forms a tufted *bush* about 0.5 m high; *branches* divergent; *prickles* unequal, short, almost straight. *Leaflets* 5–7 (–9), round or elliptic, simply dentate; petiole glabrous, normally unarmed; stipules narrow, acute. *Flowers* delicate pink, faintly scented, solitary on the laterals; pedicels glabrous or hispid, often both types occurring from one root. Otherwise it differs from the common Pimpernel Rose with single red flowers only by the more or less double corolla of 6–7 series of *petals*, and the much lower habit. *Heps* the size of a small wild cherry, red at first, blackening at maturity.

Descemet, one of our most distinguished growers, obtained the seeds and distributed this rose, which is notable for its elegance and the profusion of blooms in spring. His plant died after three years in a hard winter but was replaced from Brisset's garden in Paris in 1811. It is readily propagated by grafting, preferably as a cleft graft. It grows slowly and produces few suckers. It is still a rarity, although the double white-flowered cultivar is common.

Rosa Pimpinellifolia rubra
(*Flore multiplici.*)

Rosier Pimprenelle rouge.
(*Variété à fleurs doubles.*)

P. Redouté pinx.   Imprimerie de Remond   Chapuy sculp.

ROSA BIFERA ALBA
'WHITE FOUR-SEASONS ROSE'

Branches diffuse, almost tortuous, glandular hispid; *prickles* straight or slightly curved. *Leaflets* 5, round or elliptic, uniformly dentate, upperside delicate green, underside and margins paler and tomentose; petiole hispid, with small yellowish prickles; stipules long, denticulate and villous at the edges. *Flowers* terminal, 3 or more together, subcorymbose, erect, double, with a characteristic sweet perfume; pedicels hispid, prickly; *receptacles* decurrent with the pedicels, funnel-shaped; *sepals* 3 pinnatifid and 2 simple, glandular with ciliate margins; *petals* 6- or 10-seriate, almost pure white, those at the centre cupped and crumpled, covering over the stamen rudiments. *Heps* (from those flowers which are not totally sterilised by doubling) very elongate ovoid.

For a long while a rarity, this shrub is now found in almost all gardens. As in all *biferas*, flowers appear early and again in the autumn, often up to the frosts, especially if during July one prunes and defoliates the shrub and waters during drought. This is the way gardeners persuade the roses to bloom in August for the Feast of Our Lady. They obtain them again in winter by placing the same rose plants in a frame (De Launay). We might add that Fion, a Parisian nurseryman, cultivates roses with such art and success that there is no season of the year when they fail to furnish him with an abundant and useful harvest. Thus the roses we see each year in early April in the Paris Flower Market are the produce of frames, forced more than a month early by the skill of our ingenious nurserymen.

The cultivar illustrated here is more delicate and less vigorous than other *biferas*. It needs a good soil and a favourable situation. Grafted on the hedge rose it produces a fine effect but does not live long, so should be often renewed.

Rosa Bifera alba.   *Rosier des quatre Saisons à fleurs blanches.*

P.J. Redouté pinx.   Imprimerie de Remond.   Bessin sculp.

ROSA INDICA CRUENTA
'BLOOD-RED CHINA ROSE'

Shrub about 0.6 m high or more; *stems* glabrous, green; *prickles* sparse, hooked, reddish, little dilated at the base. *Leaflets* 3–5 (–7), oblong ovate, rounded at the base, acute at the tip, upperside green, underside paler; simply dentate, teeth sometimes reddish; petiole a little glandular at the base, armed with hooked prickles which often extend up to the midrib of the odd leaflet; stipules edged with stalked glands. *Flowers* often very large, terminal, solitary on young plants but in threes subcorymbosely on adults; *receptacles* subglobose, glabrous, pedicels long, glandular hispid; *sepals* fairly short, acute, 2 entire and 3 simply pinnate; pedicels, receptacles and sepals flushed red on parts exposed to the sun; *petals* 5–6-seriate, red-purple or blood-coloured, somewhat velvety, irregularly notched; *styles* bright red.

Imported from China by T. Evans and flowered in England for the first time in Colville's Nursery about 1810. This most beautiful of the purple Chinas blooms in the orangery or a very sheltered frame in early spring, the flowers being outstanding for their volume and perfection of form. It can be successfully grafted on *canina* or the Common China, but in this case the blooms will be smaller and appear only at the end of June.

Rosa Indica Cruenta.

Rosier du Bengale a fleurs pourpre-de-sang.

P. J. Redouté pinx.   Imprimerie de Rémond   Langlois sculp.

ROSA RUBIGINOSA CRETICA
'CRETAN ROSE'

Tufted *bush* 0.6–0.9 m tall; *prickles* hooked, much dilated at the base. *Leaflets* 5–7, apple-scented when rubbed, simply serrate, underside and margins with hairs and sessile viscous glands; petiole villous, glandular, with small yellow recurved prickles; stipules broad, spreading, pointed above, gland-edged. *Flowers* in June, 1 (–3) at the tips of the laterals, with a faint scent similar to the leaves; *receptacles* short, subglobose; pedicels elongated; both greenish glandular hispid; *sepals* longer than the bud, entire or rarely with 1–2 pinnules, spatulate, sometimes leafy at the tip, villous within, densely covered with small viscous glands outside, long persistent; *petals* 5, bright pink, yellowing towards the base, cordately notched; *styles* villous, a little exserted. *Heps* hemispherical, red and losing some of their bristles when ripe.

Indigenous to the Greek islands, the Cretan rose was found by Demetrius in Corfu, where the heps are used for jam and confectioneries. It is very similar to the Clemence Eglantine which is, however, shorter and more spreading, more or less glabrous, with flowers always solitary on very short pedicels. This is a plant for the botanical garden, and hence little distributed. Tournefort knew it, having been sent it by Du Pont.

Rosa Rubiginosa Cretica.

Rosier de Crete.

P. J. Redouté pinx.

Imprimerie de Remond.

Langlois sculp

ROSA TURBINATA
'FRANKFORT ROSE'

Bush 1.5–1.8 m tall; current *branches* glaucescent and almost glabrous; adult *stems* armed with a fair number of scattered, unequal *prickles*, some straight, others recurved, which are densely crowded on all old wood; flowering branches quite glabrous. *Leaflets* 5, ovate, subacute, upperside green, underside tomentose; simply dentate; petioles villous; stipules slightly glandular. *Flowers* 1–3 at the branch tips, subcorymbose, with a soft, pleasant scent; pedicels glandular hispid in youth; bracts basal, ovate acuminate, quite entire, ciliate at the margins like the stipules; *receptacles* top-shaped, glabrous, sometimes dark red and armed at the base with small reflexed hairs tipped with brown glands; *sepals* shorter than the petals, tomentose within, glandular outside, acuminate, entire or more often with broad-based linear appendages; *corolla* always double but never full, approaching the volume of *R. centifolia* but darker; *styles* very numerous, villous.

A native of Northern Europe, this is grown in gardens under the names 'Top-shaped Rose', 'Frankfort Rose' and so on. According to De Candolle it is intermediate in habit between *R. villosa* and *R. centifolia*, although very different from either. The flowers often open imperfectly, as do all the roses with turbinate receptacles: *R. sulfurea* and its cultivar 'Yellow Pompon', *R. alpina turbinata*, *R. fraxinifolia*, *R. sanguisorbaefolia* and so on.

Rosa Turbinata.

Rosier de Francfort.

P. J. Redouté pinx.

Imprimerie de Rémond

Bessin sculp.

ROSA LEUCANTHA
'WHITE-FLOWERED ROSE'

Tufted *bush* 2–3.6 m high; stem *prickles* sparse, stout, hooked, a lively red, the principal ones paired or 5–6 in whorls near the insertion of young branches, especially on current, non-flowering shoots; prickles on adult stems fewer, grey, weaker. *Leaflets* 5–7, ovate acute in the upper branches, subobtuse in the lower branches, simply dentate, upperside scarcely pubescent, underside and margins villous; petiole covered in weak, recumbent hairs and yellow, recurved, almost always hooked prickles; stipules large, pointed, tomentose, margins with sessile glands and very minute down. *Flowers* large, faintly scented, lateral and terminal, corymbose at the branch tips; *receptacles* oblong, glabrous; pedicels also glabrous, very short, with ovate acute bracts, ciliate and gland-edged; *sepals* villous within, glabrous outside, 3 pinnatifid and 2 simple; *petals* 5, white, faintly flushed pink in the upper part at anthesis, yellowing towards the base, cordately notched; *styles* distinct, bristly.

Apparently a white-flowered modification of *R. collina* D.C. non Jacq., as shown by the leaflets tomentose underneath and receptacle and pedicel glabrous. Not to be confused with *R. canina*, whose leaves are glabrous on both sides, nor *R. montana*, whose leaflets are bidentate, glabrous and gland-edged. Desvaux considers all these as varieties of *R. canina*. *R. leucantha* approaches *R. brevistyla candida* D.C., but this has glabrous leaflets and coherent styles, and *R. dumetorum* Thuill., but this has soft pink flowers, fewer prickles, leaflets less white underneath and styles more capitate.

It is found in the undergrowth at the foot of a hill beside the road to Meudon at Bellevue. L. Deslongchamps saw it near Dreux and was first to publish it. His taxon, smaller in all its parts (*R. obtusifolia* or *canina obtusifolia* Desv.) was found at Belleville and has smaller, more generally obtuse leaflets and fewer, corymbose flowers. Both roses flower in June.

Rosa Leucantha.   *Rosier a fleurs blanches.*

P. J. Redouté pinx.   Imprimerie de Remond   Chapuy Sculp.

ROSA FOETIDA
'FOUL-FRUITED ROSE'

Shrub 1.5–1.8 m high; *stems* glabrous, with long, almost straight, scattered reddish prickles, especially on the barren shoots, sub-geminate when near the stipules. *Leaflets* 5–7(–9), upperside glabrous, underside pubescent, base often cordate, apex pointed, biserrate; petioles villous, glandular, with small recurved prickles which often extend up to the midrib of the terminal leaflet; stipules diaphanous, acute, glandular. *Flowers* rather small, almost scentless, 1(–3) on the laterals; *receptacles* small, elongated ovoid; pedicels and pinnatifid *sepals* glandular and aciculate; *petals* 5, delicate pink at first, rapidly fading; *styles* short, free, a little villous. *Heps* ovoid, almost always aciculate, rarely glabrous, red tinged with orange at maturity, very foetid when bruised.

Discovered by Bastard on the banks of the Loire, this rose should probably be included in the Series Collina when rose classification becomes more stabilised. It resembles *R. tomentosa* a little in habit, but that has the leaves hairy on both sides and the prickles broader based. According to Bastard it is very rare both in the wild and in cultivation. It was introduced by Le Meunier, and should not be confused with *R. foetida* Herrm. or Allion.

Rosa fœtida.

Rosier a fruit fetide.

P. J. Redouté pinx. Imprimerie de Remond Chapuy sculp

ROSA CINNAMOMEA FLORE SIMPLICI
'SINGLE MAY ROSE'

Bush 1.2–1.5 m tall; flowering *branches* smooth and quite glabrous; adult *stems* with many, densely crowded, short, almost straight *prickles* on their lower parts. *Leaflets* 7, ovate, simply dentate, upperside glabrous, underside slightly pubescent, especially on the ribs. *Flowers* scented, several together at the branch tips, subcorymbose; *receptacles* subglobose, glabrous; pedicel also glabrous; *sepals* very long; *petals* 5, cordately notched, more or less reddened according to exposure of the shrub; *stigmas* aggregated into a head.

This rose grows spontaneously in Southern Europe and flowers in May. The Cinnamon roses have undergone many modifications as a result of cultivation and some botanists have recognised these as species. However, the characters on which they are founded are of little value, and all are here reunited under *R. cinnamomea*.

Rosa Cinnamomea flore simplici.   *Rosier de Mai à fleurs simples.*

P. J. Redouté pinx.   Imprimerie de Remond.   Charlin sculp.

ROSA GALLICA VERSICOLOR
'ROSA MUNDI' (Lit. 'STRIPED ROSE OF FRANCE')

Bush 0.6–0.9 m high; *stems* bristly with unequal *prickles*, the longer hooked and the shorter almost straight. *Leaflets* 7, oblong, acute, rounded at the base, upperside glabrous, underside tomentose; glandular on the margins; petioles villous, sometimes a little prickly; stipules simple, acute, edged with sessile glands. *Flowers* faintly scented, mostly in threes at the branch tips; *receptacles* subglobose, hispid; pedicels hispid; bracts 2, oval, most often leafy and glandular like the stipules; *sepals* short, 3 pinnatifid and 2 simple, acute, downy within, downy mixed with sessile glands outside; *corolla* always semi-double, never full; *petals* delicate pink striped with more or less bright red. *Heps* globose, reddish.

The variegations which distinguish this cultivar often disappear, and it is not rare to see in one year variegated blooms followed by those of one colour only. This tendency to revert requires that the plant should be frequently renewed by grafting.

It is known in France as 'Provins Panaché' or 'Provins Oeillet' and in England as 'Rosamunde' after the beautiful and intelligent mistress of Henry II. 'Rosamunde' derives from the German Rosen, a rose, and mund, a mouth, or 'Mouth-of-rose'.

Rosa gallica versicolor flowers better in shade than in full sun. It does very well grafted, but own-root shrubs give larger and more brilliant blooms.

Rosa Gallica Versicolor.   *Rosier de France a fleurs panachées.*

P. J. Redouté pinx.   Imprimerie de Rémond   Langlois sculp.

ROSA DAMASCENA VARIEGATA
'YORK AND LANCASTER ROSE'

Adult *stems* with few, sparse, recurved *prickles* little dilated at the base; flowering *branches* bristly with unequal, reddish prickles, some very weak, others stronger. *Leaflets* 5 or 7, acute, ovate, upperside bright green, underside and margins paler and pubescent simply and not deeply dentate, entire at the base; petioles villous, covered with small sessile reddish glands; stipules slightly tomentose. *Flowers* sweetly scented, many together in a lax terminal panicle; *receptacles* attenuated at both ends, a little swollen midway, together with the elongated pedicel bristly from many viscous, scented glands; bracts 2, acute, ovate, pubescent on the margins; *sepals* 3 pinnatifid, 2 simple, elongated spatulate, downy within, glandular outside; *petals* 4–5-seriate, those at the centre cupped and crumpled, most often white, spotted or striped with pink, the same bush often giving all pink and all white blooms.

This beautiful cultivar, known in gardens as 'York and Lancaster Rose', 'Striped Four-Seasons Rose' or 'Striped Damask', was propagated by Du Pont who had it from England under the name *R. damascena bicolor*. It should not be confused with *R. damascena felicitas* ('La Felicité') or with *R. gallica versicolor*, as Roessig incorrectly calls it. It is still rather rare in gardens, and needs a sheltered site. It can be grown on its own roots, but does better grafted on *canina*.

Rosa Damascena Variegata.   *Rosier d'Yorck et de Lancastre.*

P. J. Redouté pinx.   Imprimerie de Rémond   Bessin sculp.

ROSA RUBIGINOSA 'ZABETH'
'QUEEN ELISABETH'S SWEETBRIAR'

Bush 0.6–0.9 m high; *stems* glabrous, green; *prickles* long, recurved, almost absent from the flowering shoots. *Leaflets* oblong ovate, acute at both ends, upperside glabrous, underside and margins tomentose and with very numerous sessile viscous glands; petiole with small greenish prickles, similarly glandular; stipules acute, quite entire, gland-edged. *Flowers* lateral and terminal, subumbellate; *receptacles* globose, like the pedicels glabrous or sometimes puberulent; all lateral pedicels with small, ovate, acute, glandular bracteoles; peduncular bracts more or less leafy; *sepals* 3 pinnatifid and 2 simple, in general acute, some spatulate or leafy at the tip; *corolla* medium-sized; *petals* 2–3-seriate, pink whitening towards the base, the innermost a little crumpled; *styles* villous, slightly more exserted than in other rubiginosas. *Heps* globose, bright red, crowned by the persistent sepals.

This resembles *Rosa sepium* in the arrangement and form of the glandular leaves, but *sepium* has scentless foliage ('Zabeth' is strongly apple-scented as typical of the *rubiginosa* Series), an ovoid or oblong receptacle, taller and more heavily armed stems and almost glabrous styles. It was propagated in France by Du Pont but has been known for a long time since, according to English tradition, it was dedicated to Queen Elisabeth.

Rosa Rubiginosa Zabeth.   *Eglantine de la Reine Elisabeth.*

P.J. Redouté pinx.   Imprimerie de Rémond   Langlois sculp

ROSA RAPA FLORE SEMIPLENO
'TURNIP ROSE'

Flowering *branches* unarmed; adult branches with a few *prickles*. *Leaflets* oblong ovate, glabrous, shining as in *R. lucida* although of a darker green. *Flowers* slow to develop and most abort; *receptacles* turbinate; *sepals* very long, incised; *petals* 4–5-seriate. *Heps* globose.

In the classification of Rosae Turbinatae given here, the group is mainly founded, so far as can be judged, on the turnip-shaped form of the receptacle as seen immediately before the opening of the flower – a constant and invariable character. The flowers of all roses of this Section rarely open well; mostly they open very badly.

Rosa Rapa. *Rosier Turneps.*

P.J. Redouté *pinx.* Imprimerie de Remond Charlin *sculp.*

ROSA ANDEGAVENSIS
'ANJOU ROSE'

Bush 2.4–3 m high; *prickles* rather sparse, small and hooked on adult branches, almost straight on flowering shoots. *Leaflets* (5–)7, ovate acute, quite glabrous; teeth simple, unusually far apart; petioles scabrous to prickly or most often glabrous; stipules gland-edged. *Flowers* slightly strawberry-scented, pale pink aging to white, (1–)2–3 at the branch tips; *receptacles* and pedicels more or less glandular hispid, rarely glabrous; *sepals* 3 pinnatifid and 2 simple, downy within and on the margins, covered outside with shortly stalked glands, pubescent; *petals* 5, cordately notched; *styles* short, distinct, pubescent. *Heps* finally ovoid, with the characteristic glandular hairs of the species at maturity.

Differs from *R. canina* only by the hispid receptacle and pedicel as well as the simple serration; *R. andegavensis* also resembles Bellard's *R. glandulosa*, but that has constantly solitary blooms of a lively red colour, and bidentate leaflets. It was discovered by Leman and first published by Bastard. It is common throughout France, and many varieties could be set up according to the more or less glaucous leaves, smaller leaflets or density of bristles on receptacles and pedicels.

Rosa Andegavensis.

Rosier d'Anjou

P. Redouté pinx.   Imprimerie de Rémond   Chapuy

ROSA CENTIFOLIA BIPINNATA
'CELERY-LEAVED ROSE'

Somewhat tufted *bush* scarcely 0.5 m high; *prickles* fine, unequal, recurved, mixed with stiff glandular hairs; *leaves* bipinnate or twice winged with soft almost reniform leaflets, deeply bidentate, upperside glabrous, underside slightly tomentose; often partially flushed with red as is the petiole. *Flowers* rather beautiful and strongly perfumed, 2–3 at the branch tips; *calyx*, pedicels and *corolla* identical to those of common *centifolia*, the prototype of this cultivar.

This is less in demand for its bloom than for the singular foliage which is the outcome of a vegetative monstrosity. Du Pont perpetuated it by grafting and made it available 12–15 years ago. The wavy, crisped leaflets resemble those of the gooseberry, whence the garden names *Rosa crispa*, 'Crinkled Rose', 'Gooseberry-leaved Rose', 'Parsley-leaved Rose' and, most generally, 'Celery-leaved Rose'. The foliage tends to revert continually to the ancestral form, especially in good soil, and it is not rare to find bipinnate and *centifolia*-type leaves on the same plant, or complete reversion to the latter. Frequent grafting is therefore necessary to preserve it. Once common, it has now become very rare, perhaps because of extreme susceptibility to aphids which make the flower unsightly. It can be obtained on its own roots only by layers, in which state it grows slowly unless in a moist soil and very favourable position. Grafted on *canina* it grows vigorously, and is best left alone – we have seen fine plants perish as a result of over-attention.

Rosa Centifolia Bipinnata.   *Rosier a feuilles de Celeri.*

P. J. Redouté pinx.   Imprimerie de Rémond.   Langlois sculp.

ROSA COLLINA FASTIGIATA
'FLAT-FLOWERED HILL ROSE'

Shrub 2.1–2.4 m high; *prickles* stout, hooked, much dilated at the base; young *branches* glabrous, a little reddish. *Leaflets* 5 or 7, ovate-lanceolate, simply dentate, upperside glossy, underside and margins tomentose; petioles pubescent, with small prickles extending sometimes up to the midrib of the odd leaflet. *Flowers* almost scentless, subumbellate; *receptacles* ovoid, glabrous; pedicels all the same length, glandular hispid; *sepals* 3 pinnatifid and 2 simple; *petals* 5, soft pink; *styles* free, glabrous.

The many varieties of *Rosa collina* have in common simply dentate leaflets with glabrous uppersides and tomentose undersides and margins – sufficient to distinguish them from other wild species with which they are frequently confused. *R. canina* is distinct by the more rounded leaflets glabrous on both sides and sometimes bidentate. *R. villosa* has the leaflets tomentose on both sides. *R. andegavensis* has the receptacle bristly and the leaflets glabrous. *R. montana* has bidentate leaflets with the upperside glabrous and glands only on the margins. *R. sepium* has bidentate leaflets covered in glands on the underside and margins, smaller in general than those of *collina*.

Rosa Collina fastigiata.

Rosier Nivelle.

P. J. Redouté pinx.

Imprimerie de Rémond.

Chapuy sculp.

ROSA SEMPERVIRENS GLOBOSA
'ROUND-FRUITED EVERGREEN ROSE'

Stems to 4.5 m tall, climbing over bushes to the tops of large trees in woods and parks; *branches* diffuse, green, glabrous; *prickles* short, hooked, yellowish. *Leaflets* 3–5(–7), firm, glossy, acute, finely and simply dentate; petiole with small prickles; stipules denticulate. *Flowers* scented, (1–)3–4 at the branch tips; *receptacles* globose or subglobose, hispid like the pedicels and sepals; bracts 2, elongated, acute; *petals* 5, white, cordate; *styles* coherent, shortly exserted in a bristly column. *Heps* persisting for part of the winter, small, globose, red.

Only the subpersistent foliage differentiates this from *R. moschata*. All varieties of *R. sempervirens* come from Italy, mainly the Florence area, where they bloom almost throughout the year. In the climate of Paris and N. France, however, own-root plants bloom with difficulty, especially if pruned. The petals are made into a supposed purgative medicine used by the people of Tuscany, although probably in minute doses.

Rosa Semper-Virens globosa.   *Rosier grimpant a fruits globuleux.*

P.J. Redouté pinx.   Imprimerie de Rémond   Chapuy sculp.

ROSA GALLICA PURPUREA VELUTINA PARVA
'VAN EEDEN'S ROSE'

Shrub with basal non-rooting suckers 0.3–0.6 m long; *prickles* unequal, fairly numerous and almost straight, sparse on the flowering shoots. *Leaflets* ovate-oblong, rounded at the base, acute, upperside green, underside slightly tomentose; bidentate; petiole villous, with very small straight prickles; stipules slightly denticulate, gland-edged; pedicels villous; *receptacles* rounded; *sepals* short, pointed, quite entire, villous within, a little hispid outside as is the receptacle. *Flowers* 3–4 at the tips of the laterals, medium-sized; *petals* 3-seriate, brilliant purple on opening and with an admirable violet, velvety look from the play of light, enhanced by the golden stamens at the centre; *styles* villous, almost tufted.

This magnificent *gallica* was obtained from seed by Van Eeden, a nurseryman of Harlem, who enriched the Malmaison garden with it in 1810. All the arts of the painter cannot render correctly the *gallica* roses, of which there are almost 500: their colours cover most of the hues shown in Newton's table of colours. After the death of Josephine, this lovely rose disappeared from Malmaison, and is still unknown on its own roots. It survives grafted in a few private gardens, but loses its prostrate habit. However, grafting if anything increases the bulk of the flowers and their brilliance. As in all *gallicas* the petals finally blacken before falling – the explanation of the so-called "black rose". It is easily obtained on its own roots by earthing up the prostrate stems, and is undemanding, although one should resist the urge to straighten up these naturally creeping suckers.

Rosa Gallica Purpurea Velutina, Parva.

Rosier de Van-Eeden.

P.J. Redouté pinx.

Imprimerie de Remond

Langlois sculp.

ROSA GALLICA REGALIS
'ROYAL HIGHNESS PROVINS ROSE'

Rather tufted *bush* 0.5–0.8 m high; *prickles* of different lengths, more or less closely set. *Leaflets* 5, ovate, thick, rugose, upperside green, underside and margins tomentose; petioles villous, mostly prickly; stipules large, denticulate. *Flowers* littles cented, 3–4 at the branch tips; pedicels and *receptacles* glandular hairy; *sepals* 3 pinnatifid and 2 simple, pointed or spatulate, covered in similar hairs outside, whitish woolly within; *corolla* semi-double; *petals* 4–5-seriate, darker pink than those of common *centifolia*; *stamens* few, some petaloid and crumpled; *styles* long, subfasciculate.

Rosa Gallica Regalis.   *Rosier Grandeur Royale.*

P.J. Redouté pinx.   Imprimerie de Remond   Bessin sculp.

ROSA ORBESSANEA [Thory sp.n.]
'ORBESSAN ROSE'

Tufted *shrub* up to 0.5 m tall; *branches* bristly from numerous, unequally long, densely packed prickles. *Leaflets* 5, 7 or 9, elliptic, glabrous, upperside green, underside paler; simply and rather deeply dentate; petiole villous, glandular and minutely prickly. *Flowers* delicate pink, semi-double, fragrant, medium-sized, 2–3 at the tips of the laterals; pedicels densely covered in spiniform hairs; *receptacles* turbinate, compressed towards the top, glabrous, wine-coloured; *sepals* glabrous and wine-coloured outside, villous inside, elongated, pointed or spatulate. *Heps* subglobose.

One of the group of roses with turbinate receptacles – see p. 8 of this volume for differential characters. It is little distributed as yet, and we have seen it only in the Sèvres nurseries where it originated. Its demands only ordinary care and excels when grafted on the wild briar, especially if sheltered to encourage well-formed blooms. It is normally covered with buds, but opens only some of them. It is dedicated to Anne-Marie d'Aignant, Marquess of Orbessan, author of the only worthwhile publication on roses since Rosenberg.

Rosa Orbessanea.

Rosier d'Orbessan.

P.J. Redouté pinx.

Imprimerie de Remond.

Lemaire sculp.

ROSA RUBIGINOSA NEMORALIS [Thory var.n.]
'WILD ROSE OF THE WOODS'

Shrub 1.8–2.4 m tall; *prickles* fairly stout, hooked, remote, sparse; young *branches* and stem tips unarmed. *Leaflets* 5(–7), pale green, elliptic, pointed, rounded at the base, irregularly dentate, pubescent on both sides and underside covered with numerous viscid glands; petiole villous, with some small, hooked prickles; stipules acute, slightly denticulate at the tip. *Flowers* 1(–3), subcorymbose on the tips of the laterals; pedicels glandular hispid; *receptacles* ovoid, similarly but less densely armed; *sepals* longer than the petals, falling before the hep ripens; *petals* 5, very small, pale pink becoming yellowish towards the base, cordately notched. *Heps* ovoid, red, retaining some bristles.

This is strongly related to Rau's *R. rubiginos* γ, which is also very small-flowered. It belongs with those roses having hispid pedicels and receptacles, but is distinct by the unarmed young branches and stem tips, clear green leaflets and tiny flowers, thus constituting a variety of *rubiginosa* but insufficient to rank as a separate species. It was found in dry, stony woods near Malmedy by Mlle Marie-Anne Libert, although not commonly.

Rosa Rubiginosa nemoralis.　　　*L'Eglantine des bois.*

P. J. Redouté pinx.　　　Imprimerie de Remond　　　Chapuy sculp.

ROSA INDICA PUMILA FLORE SIMPLICI
'DWARF SINGLE CHINA ROSE'

Scarcely 0.3 m high; *prickles* sparse, reddish, almost straight. *Leaflets* 3 or 5, glabrous, acute, finely and simply dentate; upperside bright green, underside paler, base rounded; petiole slightly pubescent, with small hooked prickles extending up to the midrib of the odd leaflet; stipules narrow, pointed, gland-edged. *Flowers* small, almost always solitary at the branch tips; pedicels thin, with glandular hairs near the top; *sepals* simple or rarely with 1–2 pinnules; *petals* 5, white flushed with pink, rounded; *receptacles* oblong-ovoid, almost glabrous, greenish; bracts 2, small, opposite, ciliate; *stamens* long, twisted and incurving over the styles. *Heps* ovoid, clear red.

Rosa indica pumila is a derivative of this rose, are distinct only by its unarmed laterals and double flowers. Both alike in habit, the ease with which they strike from cuttings and flower straight away, and the type of culture needed. It is close to *R. semperflorens minima* var. γ, 'Miss Lawrance's Rose', which differs only by the stalked glands covering the stems. It is a rose for the orangery, and heps take two seasons to ripen achenes.

Rosa Indica Pumila,
(flore simplici).

Petit Rosier du Bengale,
(a fleurs simples).

P. J. Redoute pinx.   Imprimerie de Remond   Chapuy sculp.

ROSA LONGIFOLIA
'PEACH-LEAVED ROSE'

Stem almost unarmed, long and tall in the East Indies where it grows, but dwarf and weakly in the climate of France; *branches* glabrous; *prickles* few, sparse, reddish, hooked, sometimes geminate. *Leaflets* 5, acuminate, 4–5(–10) cm long, the odd leaflet always longer than the others, glabrous, simply dentate, teeth distant; petiole with glandular hairs and small prickles; stipules narrow, pointed, scarcely glandular. *Flowers* (1–)3–4, subumbellate at the branch tips; pedicels fairly long, sometimes with stalked glands towards the top; bracts very narrow, gland-edged; *receptacles* elongated ovoid, glabrous; *sepals* simple, various – some pointed, others spatulate or leafy; *petals* 10–12, unequal, soft pink sometimes variegated with white spots, rounded or notched, some elongated, others crumpled and curled in the centre of the flower. *Heps* ovoid, reddish.

This modification of the China Rose belongs in the *indica* group, notwithstanding Willdenow and his followers who make it a separate species. It differs in having glands at the top of the pedicel and glabrous leaves; otherwise it has all the characters of *R. indica*: the same stamens, the deflexing sepals after anthesis, the same ease of rooting from cuttings and almost perennial blooming. Its affinity with *R. indica* is confirmed by Bounder of Dijon who obtained an almost identical rose in 1810 from seed of the Common China save that the petals were strap like, similar to the rays of a sunflower.

This rose is not common and needs an orangery. Nurseries know it as *R. persicifolia*. It should not be confused with the 'Hemp-leaved Rose' *R. alba cymbaefolia* var. x.

Rosa Longifolia

Rosier a feuilles de Pêcher

P.J. Redouté pinx.   Imprimerie de Remond.   Charlin sculp.

ROSA GALLICA PURPUREO-VIOLACEA MAGNA
'BISHOP ROSE'

Stems somewhat reddish, with recurved prickles; *branches* diffuse, with fairly numerous, small, unequal, almost straight, ephemeral *prickles*, densely packed, especially at the extremities of the plant. *Leaflets* 5, firm, rounded ovate, dark green, upperside glabrous, underside tomentose; petioles villous, glandular, with many, small, inclined prickles. *Flowers* faintly scented, 1–3 at the branch tips; pedicels long, hispid; *receptacles* rounded, almost glabrous, sometimes glandular: *sepals* pinnatifid, glabrous or glandular hairy; *corolla* large; *petals* 2–3-seriate, a fine purple-violet, broad, cordately notched or subcrenate; *styles* fasciculate.

This beautiful and long-know cultivar of the Provins Rose is grown in almost all gardens. It is the parent of many violet-colored derivatives, all notable for their brilliant colours and themselves having given rise to seedlings of different shades, more or less double, some striped or spotted with white, others white towards the base, and all very fine. Florists have preferred the single or semi-double to the double cultivars. Botanists, however, disdain them, considering them degenerate and a sign of the impermanence of species in *Rosa*.

Rosa Gallica.
(Purpuro-violacea magna.)

Rosier Eveque.

P. J. Redouté pinx.   Imprimerie de Remond   Langlois sculp.

ROSA ACIPHYLLA
'CUSPIDATE ROSE'

Shrub 0.6–0.8 m high; *branches* straight, stiff, dark brown veering towards green; *prickles* few, recurved, almost solitary; laterals short, densely crowded. *Leaflets* 5 or 7, glabrous, green on both surfaces, oblong-lanceolate, cuspidate, unequally dentate, each tooth tipped with a gland which is sessile on the large teeth and stalked on the smaller; petioles often unarmed, upperside pubescent, underside glabrous; stipules small, narrow, pointed, gland-edged. *Flowers* 1–4, subumbellate at the tips of the laterals; pedicels weak, very short; bracts oblong, acute; *receptacles* globose, glabrous; *sepals* acute, appendiculate, villous on the inside and margins, glabrous outside, longer than the 5 very small, pink-flushed white *petals*. *Heps* globose, glabrous.

Rosa aciphylla grows near Würzburg where it was discovered on a calcareous hill by Heller and published by Rau with a good illustration by Sturm. The name *aciphylla* alludes to the pointed leaves. It occurs only in stony waste places and the heps ripen with difficulty even in the wild. In gardens it flowers well but is barren most years. At first glance it looks unlike any other rose, but it seems to be merely a modification of *R. canina* with ovate leaflets and ovoid receptacle. Rau confirms this following his description of *R. canina* var. β *ramosissima*, which is transitional to *R. aciphylla*.

Rosa acuphylla.

Rosier cuspidé.

P. J. Redouté pinx.

Imprimerie de Rémond.

Chapuy sculp.

ROSA MALMUNDARIENSIS
'MALMEDY ROSE'

Shrub 1.8–2.1 m tall; *prickles* sparse, straight or recurved, much dilated at the base, often paired near the stipules. *Leaflets* 5–(7–9), ovate to subrotund in the wild, oblong in cultivation, glabrous, unequally dentate with many glands on the teeth, upperside green, underside paler; petiole glandular hairy and almost always with small hooked prickles; stipules broad, acute, gland-edged. *Flowers* 1–3 at the tips of the laterals; pedicels glabrous or very rarely a little glandular; bracts 2, opposite, fairly large, acute, sometimes denticulate above, sheathing at the base; *receptacles* ovoid, glabrous; *sepals* appendiculate, glandular outside, downy within; *petals* 5, very pale pink, cordately notched; *styles* villous; *stigmas* aggregated in a head. *Heps* rather large, subglobose, red.

Found by Le Jeune in the mountains near Malmedy, this rose is distinct from all others in the wild by the leaflets being glabrous on both surfaces but glandular only on the margins. This is the prime character of *R. montana* Willd., of which it is certainly a modification. *R. canina* shares the glabrous leaflets but is rarely bidentate and not gland-edged. Nor can it be referred to *R. sepium*, whose long, narrow leaflets are glandular on the margin and underside. The Rosae Montanae are found in mountains, woods and dry places mainly in the North of France.

Rosa Malmundariensis.   *Rosier de Malmedy.*

P. J. Redouté pinx.   Imprimerie de Rémond.   Langlois sculp.

ROSA INDICA MULTIPETALA
'HUNDRED-PETALLED CHINA ROSE'

Tufted *bush* 0.9–1.2 m tall or more in cool, humid soils; *branches* green, glabrous; *prickles* strong, hooked, much dilated at the base, reddish. *Leaflets* 5, rounded ovate, shining, firm, often undulate, curiously pointed, upperside green, underside paler; petioles tomentose, with numerous, small, hooked prickles the same colour as those on the stems. *Flowers* 2–3 at the branch tips, faintly scented, double, but a little less so than in *R. centifolia*, pink, a little darker pink than in the Common China; peduncles glabrous; pedicels slightly tomentose; *receptacles* ovoid, glabrous; *sepals* 5, almost entire, always reflexed after expansion, glabrous outside, downy within; *corolla* 35-40 mm in diameter; *petals* many-seriate, cordately notched, those at the centre curled and crumpled, scarcely allowing those stamens not converted to petals to be seen; bud bright red before opening; the later blooms, except in very favourable circumstances, rarely open well.

Known in the trade as 'Hundred-petalled Bengal', 'Large Bengal', 'Double Bengal' and 'Wavy-leaved Bengal', this can be propagated only by suckers, cuttings or grafting. Like the Common Bengal or China Roses it succeeds well outdoors given a sheltered aspect and above all a moist soil, but is susceptible to black spot like all other China Rose. Branches thus affected should be removed immediately, but as the largest are difficult to cut out with a pruning knife we recommend Parmentier's secateur and Regnier's clippers. The Common China and the rose figured here are the only ones of their group truly acclimatised to France and able to resist the cold outdoors. We could cite gardens where they have thus survived more than 20 years by pruning away black spot. All the other Chinas languish and die, even if covered. A peaty soil, an orangery, and above all light and ventilation are the best means to keep them.

Rosa Indica.

Rosier du Bengale (Cent feuille).

P. J. Redouté pinx.

Imprimerie de Rémond

Charlin sculp.

ROSA INDICA PANNOSA
'VELVET CHINA ROSE'

Shrub scarcely 0.5 m high. *Flowers* purple with paler stripes; *petals* concave, undulate, crumpled or variously formed, cinnamon-scented but only at the time of opening.

This is very common in nurseries as the 'Tattered Rose', 'Purple-striped Bengal', 'Velvet Rose' and 'Cinnamon-scented Rose'. It was raised from seed a dozen years ago by Gauché, a gardener-florist of Paris, who introduced it.

We have brought together under a single Section, the China Roses, not only the varieties of *R. indica,* but many others segregated as distinct species. All except *R. indica vulgaris* and *R. indica multipetala* need an orangery in winter and peaty soil. They propagate readily from cuttings. All are more or less continuously in flower, although their hybrids flower but once each year: 'Philip Noisette' (*R. indica* x *moschata*), 'Boursault Rose' (*R. indica* x *alpina*), and so on.

Rosa Indica.　　　　　　　　*La Bengale bichonne.*

P. J. Redouté pinx.　　　　　Imprimerie de Rémond　　　　　Langlois sculp.

ROSA TOMENTOSA
'DOWNY ROSE'

Stems 1.2–1.5 m high; *prickles* long, almost straight, a little compressed at the base. *Leaflets* smaller than those of *R. villosa vulgaris*, with both surfaces covered in numerous, soft, accumbent hairs. *Flowers* pale pink. Differs from *R. villosa* only by the more or less elongated ovoid *receptacles* and *heps*. Common in the forest of Fontainebleau, this rose was also discovered in woods at Meudon near Paris in 1817 by Mlle Joséphine Redouté, where it had escaped the notice of Thuillier who perhaps regarded it as a mere variety of *R. villosa*.

Rosa farinosa Rau is a *shrub* not above 0.9 m tall with pendent *branches; prickles* shorter and less frequent than in *R. tomentosa* and an ovoid *receptacle* flattened as are the *styles*. It is common at Würzburg where it is called 'Farinose Rose' because at a distance it looks as if the whole plant is dull white.

Rosa caucasica Marsch. has the *stems* apparently unarmed, only the petioles being prickly, bidentate *leaflets* tomentose on both surfaces and white *flowers* flushed with pink. This 'Caucasian Rose' or 'Villous Rose of Tartary' grows in Asiatic Tartary.

Rosa Tomentosa.

Rosier Cotonneux.

P. J. Redouté pinx.

Imprimerie de Rémond.

Langlois sculp.

ROSA DAMASCENA AURORA
'AURORA PONIATOWSKA ROSE'

Tufted *bush* 0.6–0.9 m high; *branches* glabrous; *prickles* slightly recurved, closely set at the base of the branches, sparse towards the tips. *Leaflets* 5, suborbicular, upperside green, underside tomentose; petioles curiously curved upwards, villous, prickly. *Flowers* many, subumbellate at the branch tips; peduncles and *receptacles* densely aciculate; *receptacles* fusiform as typical of *R. damascena; sepals* much longer than the bud, pinnatifid and much dilated at the tip, glandular outside, whitish woolly within; *corolla* fairly large; *petals* 6–7-seriate, pink veering towards yellow; *styles* in many groups.

One of the finest of all shrub roses, this is much sought after for both the fine form of the flower and its delicate colouring suggesting a sunrise – whence the names 'Rose Aurore' and 'Rose Belle Aurore'. To these we couple the name of Aurore Poniatowska, an aspiring pupil of Redouté. The plant demands a sheltered site, and gives fine blooms when grafted on wild briar. Although listed for a long time in nurserymen's catalogues, it is in comparatively few gardens. It was introduced to France from Holland at the end of the eighteenth century, and propagated by Du Pont.

Rosa Damascena aurora.   *Rosier Aurore Poniatowska.*

P. Redouté pinx.   Imprimerie de Rémond.   Chardin sculp.

ROSA BANKSIAE
'LADY BANKS'S ROSE'

Basally branched *shrub*, rambling and climbing to a great height when supported; *branches* long, whiplike, glabrous, green, unarmed. *Leaflets* (3–)5–7, elliptic ovate, glossy on both surfaces, finely and simply dentate with a glandular hair on each tooth; petiole upperside glabrous, underside with soft recumbent hairs extending to the ribs of the leaflets; stipules 2, free, setaceous, villous, acute, withering and falling early. *Flowers* small, with a sweet penetrating scent like violets, 10–20 in simple umbels on the laterals; pedicels 3–4 cm long; bracts 2, one simple, the other of 3(–5) leaflets; *receptacles* globose, glabrous like the pedicels; *sepals* short, entire, acute, glabrous outside, whitish woolly within; *petals* 4–5-seriate, pure clear white, those at the centre curled and crumpled, almost hiding the remaining stamens; *styles* short, free; *stigmas* a rather bright red.

This rose was imported from China in 1807 to England and is dedicated to Lady Banks, wife of the illustrious Banks who was one of the scientists on Captain Cook's expedition. Boursault brought it to France in 1817 and grew it planted out in peaty soil in his magnificent temperate house where it exceeded 13 m. One of its flower bouquets served as a model for this painting.

Rosa banksiae is related to *R. sempervirens globosa* Thory and *R. sempervirens microphylla* D.C., but differs in its glabrous stems, pedicels and receptacles; large umbels; free, filiform, caducous stipules; no bracteoles and free styles.

Pot plants raised by Cels and Noisette have done badly and not flowered. It would be desirable if this could be acclimatised outdoors where it would be suitable for covering arbours, permeating them with the delicious fragrance of its blooms.

Rosa Banksiæ.   *Rosier de Lady Banks.*

P. J. Redouté pinx.   Imprimerie de Remond   Chapuy sculp.

ROSA CANDOLLEANA ELEGANS
'DE CANDOLLE'S ROSE'

Shapely shrub 1.2–1.5 m tall; *stems* reddish brown, with apices and current growths bristly with numerous, small, very dense, almost equal *prickles;* adult *branches* with similar prickles mixed with others longer and almost straight. *Leaflets* 5 or 7, rather small, mostly obtuse ovate but some acute ovate, unequally dentate, often purplish at the margin, upperside green, underside paler; petioles pubescent, rarely prickly; stipules spreading, denticulate. *Flowers* 2–3 at the tips of the laterals, faintly scented; pedicels and ovoid *receptacles* glabrous; *sepals* elongated, quite entire, villous within, with small sessile glands outside; *petals* 5, white ornamented outside with longitudinal bands or streaks of lively pink. *Heps* ovoid, roundish, red.

This group of roses has been dedicated to Pyr.-Aug. De Candolle, Professor of Natural History at Geneva, Director of the Botanical Garden and member of the Academy of Sciences at the same city. Three varieties are described:

R. candolleana elegans, which has similar inflorescences to *R. redutea glauca*, but that is distinguished by its long, rigid, unequal, more distant prickles, leaflets simply dentate, petals white spattered with reddish spots inside and at the tip, and especially by the general habit. *R. hispida* Poir. differs by its sparse, rigid prickles, tomentose leaflet undersides, solitary flowers and glandular hairs on pedicels and receptacles.

R. candolleana pendula, which has much larger leaflets, pale pink petals and pendent hips as in *R. alpina pendulina*. From *R. pimpinellifolia* and *R. myriacantha* this differs in having clustered flowers, bidentate leaflets, sepals longer than the buds and dissimilar prickle distribution.

R. candolleana flavescens, which is only 30–45 cm tall and has pale yellow flowers.

Rosa Candolleana Elegans.   *Rosier de Candolle.*

P.J. Redouté pinx.   Imprimerie de Rémond.   Langlois sculp.

ROSA ALBA CYMBAEFOLIA
'HEMP-LEAVED WHITE ROSE'

Bush 0.6–0.9 m tall; *branches* glabrous; *prickles* none or very few, almost straight. *Leaflets* 5, lanceolate, sometimes 7.5–10 cm long, distant, dark green, with very prominent ribs, irregularly dentate, with inrolled margins, upperside glabrous, underside more or less tomentose; petioles slightly tomentose; stipules decurrent, acute. *Flowers* mediumsized, pure white, many, subcorymbose at the branch tips; pedicels glabrous or some glandular hispid; bracts oblong ovate, much elongated; *receptacles* abruptly rounded at the base, glabrous or more often hirsute like the pedicels; *sepals* entire, acute, spatulate, almost completely glabrous outside, villous within; *petals* many-seriate, irregularly notched, those at the centre curled and crumpled. *Heps* ovoid, red, rarely maturing.

This is only a degeneration of *Rosa alba*, preserved by the nurseryman Flobert by grafting and presented to the Jardin des Plantes in Paris in 1810 by Le Pelletier as "*R. cymbaefolia*", the 'Boat-leaved Rose'. Some years ago we managed to obtain seedlings from our own plant and they reverted to *R. alba*. It also tends to revert to *R. alba* so that both types are commonly seen on the same root. It likes a light soil and frequent watering in spring.

Rosa Alba Cimbæfolia.   *Rosier blanc a feuilles de Chanvre.*

P. J. Redouté pinx.   Imprimerie de Rémond.   Bessin sculp.

ROSA SEMPERVIRENS LATIFOLIA
'BIG-LEAVED CLIMBING ROSE'

Shrub capable of great height (10 m in Du Pont's collection); *prickles* sparse, straight or recurved. *Leaflets* 5, 4–6 times larger than those of our wild *R. sempervirens*, glabrous, glossy, especially on the upperside, rounded at the base, acute, simply denticulate; petioles with hairs, glands and some small, recurved prickles; stipules decurrent, acute, denticulate and gland-edged. *Flowers* pleasantly scented, 3–6 or more, subumbellate at the tips of the laterals; pedicels long, glandular hispid, each (except the central) with 2 small bracteoles; peduncle with 2 larger bracts, sometimes leafy, at the base; *receptacles* ovoid, usually glabrous; *sepals* 3 pinnatifid and 2 simple, villous outside, woolly within and on the margins; *petals* 5, white inside, sometimes adorned on the outside with longitudinal pink stripes; *styles* united, villous (especially near the stigmas), 10–12 mm. long, presenting a form that prompted Du Pont to name this "Rosa phalloidea". *Heps* maturing with difficulty in the climate of Paris.

This rose, which is very rare in France, holds its leaves in winter as do all roses of this group. It is supposed to grow wild in Italy, having been recognised among dried specimens sent from Florence. Ours came from Du Pont a long time ago. It flowers outdoors only in a South-facing aspect and unpruned, as do all *sempervirens* roses.

Rosa sempervirens latifolia   *Rosier grimpant a grandes feuilles.*

P. J. Redouté pinx.   Imprimerie de Rémond   Langlois sculp.

ROSA CANINA NITENS
'SHINY-LEAVED DOG ROSE'

This is very common in waste places and easily distinct from other varieties of *R. canina* by its glossy foliage.

Most wild roses were included by the ancients under the name Cynorrhodon (Dog Roses), so we now propose the name Cynorrhodonenses for the whole group, characterised by leaflets glabrous on both surfaces and bracts ciliate and glandular.

The heps of these roses have many uses in domestic economy. The Germans make a faintly acid and very piquant sauce from them, similar in colour to tomato ketchup, The ancients believed the roots to be a cure for rabies.

The bedeguar or devil's pincushion occurs mainly on roses of this group: a soft, fuzzy gall caused by the Bedeguar Gall Fly. However, it does occur, although rarely, on other species.

Finally, we repeat, for those who do not already know it, the enigmatic verse referring to the five sepals of a Dog Rose:

Five brothers we: two bearded, two beardless,

and I have half a beard.

Rosa Canina nitens.   *Rosier Canin à feuilles luisantes.*

P.J. Redouté pinx.   Imprimerie de Remond   Lémaire sculp.

ROSA DAMASCENA CELSIANA
'CELS'S ROSE'

Bush 0.8–0.9 m tall; *prickles* short, unequal, the longest almost straight, with very numerous, scattered, stiff glandular bristles which readily detach leaving small blackish scars. *Leaflets* 5 or 7, ovate, simply dentate, upperside clear green, underside paler; petioles glandular, with many small reddish almost straight prickles; stipules acute, denticulate, gland-edged. *Flowers* very numerous, often 7.5 cm in diameter, perfumed, erect, subcorymbose at the branch tips; peduncles and pedicels covered in stiff, unequal, viscous stipitate glands; *receptacles* fusiform, subglabrous in the upper part, glandular below; *sepals* pinnatifid, slightly downy within, glandular outside; *petals* 5–6-seriate, cordately notched, those at the centre curled and crumpled, soft pink at anthesis but quickly fading to white so that the shrub seems covered in pink and white blooms at the same time. *Heps* rarely setting.

This is dedicated to Jacques-Martin Cels, author of learned discourses on agriculture and other subjects, who first distributed the rose to French gardens, although it had been known much earlier in Harlem and is shown in the paintings of Van Huysum. Only ordinary culture is needed, and it thrives grafted on the wild briar, but to prolong flowering it should be shaded from full sun.

Rosa Damascena.

Rosier de Cels.

P. J. Redouté pinx.

Imprimerie de Rémond

Charlin sculp.

ROSA ALPINA FLORE VARIEGATO
'VARIEGATED ALPINE ROSE'

Shrub 0.9–1.2 m high, differing from *R. alpina* only in the *petals* being attractively striped with bright red on a pink base. The rather small flowers appear in succession from early spring to the end of August, especially when it is given a northerly exposure. This modification of the Alpine Rose was introduced by Poilpré, a nurseryman of Le Mans, to Le Meunier seven to eight years ago. «Few roses» says De Candolle «are as variable as *alpina*. Most often it lacks prickles, sometimes it has some at the base, and so on. I have found so many intermediates between the varieties that it is impossible to regard them as distinct.» Desvaux has made an extensive study of them and is the main authority for their naming. All the varieties are in demand for decorating large parks, their bright reds heps persisting into winter, but in small gardens their roots are too invasive. Connoisseurs refrain from pruning, merely trimming to preserve a good shape. Experience proves the Alpine Roses to be excellent grafting stocks.

Rosa Alpina flore variegato.   *Rosier des Alpes à fleurs panachées.*

P. J. Redouté pinx.   Imprimerie de Remond.   Chapuy sculp.

ROSA POMPONIA FLORE SUBSIMPLICI
'SINGLE POMPON ROSE'

Weak *shrub* scarcely 0.5 m high, like the 'Double Pompon Rose' (Vol. 1 p. 46) but a little less prickly and with only (5–)6–7 *petals*, some distinctly pointed. *Heps* small, elongated, red, commonly abortive.

We have grown this rose since 1815 and it constantly gives blooms with 6 or 7 petals, although 5 have been seen. It was raised in 1807 by Auvé-Charpentier, a surgeon of Sablé near La Flèche. The Pompon Rose is a fertile hybrid of *R. centifolia* and *R. gallica*, regarded as a species in its own right by De Candolle but grouped among the centifolias by many authors. It differs from these by the simply dentate leaflets, prickly petioles, paired flowers and very dissimilar stature. Further common names in nurseries are 'Pygmy Pompon', 'Red Pompon', 'Alpine Pompon', 'Dijon Pompon', 'Rose de Meaux' and *Rosa meldensis*.

Rosa Pomponia flore subsimplici.   *Rosier* Pompon à fleurs presque simples.

P. J. Redouté pinx.   Imprimerie de Remond   Chapuy Sculp.

ROSA CENTIFOLIA FOLIACEA
'LEAFY ROSE'

Shrub 0.3–0.6 m high; *stems* and *foliage* similar to *centifolia*, from which it differs only by the long leafy *sepals* formed at the expense of the receptacle which is almost absent. The leafy-sepal sport has also arisen in the China Roses, the Provins Agathas and the Four Seasons Roses, and is promoted either by over-cultivation, soil quality or other growth influences. Such changes can be perpetuated by grafting.

The 'Leafy Rose' was introduced by Descemet, Professor of Agriculture and Director of the Botanical Garden and nurseries of the Tsar of Russia at Odessa. It is propagated only by grafting or layering. As grown on its own roots by Pelletier it produces many very fine blooms, but we have seen magnificent grafted specimens in Descemet's former nursery at Saint-Denis near Paris. Sometimes the flowers are proliferous and leafy at the same time. Culture is the same as for *centifolia*, pruning hard to encourage good, typical blooms:

Rosa centifolia foliacea.   *Rosier à cent feuilles, foliacé.*

P.J. Redoute pinx.   Imprimerie de Rémond   Langlois sculp.

ROSA SEPIUM ROSEA
'PINK HEDGE ROSE'

Tall, much-branched *shrub; prickles* numerous, whitish, recurved. *Leaflets* 5 or 7, usually very small, distant, acute at both ends, upperside glabrous, underside glandular; teeth glandular serrate; petioles long, glandular, prickly. *Flowers* 1–3 at the tips of the laterals; pedicels and ovoid *receptacles* glabrous; *sepals* pinnatifid; *petals* 5, pale pink at first, soon fading to white, especially on exposure to sunlight. *Heps* ovoid.

The roses of the *sepium* group are common throughout France. Some authors suppose the species to be merely a modification of *R. rubiginosa*, but this latter has shorter stems, subrotund leaflets with the upperside slightly pubescent and the underside and margins covered with viscous, apple-scented glands mixed with often rust-coloured hairs.

Rosa sepium rosea.

Rosier des hayes à fleurs roses.

P. J. Redouté pinx.   Imprimerie de Rémond.   Lemaire sculp.

ROSA PUMILA
'ROSE OF LOVE'

Subshrub 0.5–0.6 m high; *stems* simple or more often branched, glandular hispid; *prickles* straight or curved, those at the branch tips persistent, but early deciduous from the stem bases leaving numerous scars. *Leaflets* (3–)5, obtuse ovate, rarely acute ovate, firm, bidentate, gland-edged, upperside glabrous and green, underside glaucous and pubescent; petioles villous, glandular, with recurved prickles. *Flowers* 1–3 at the branch tips, fragrant; pedicels and ovoid *receptacles* glandular hairy; *sepals* lanceolate, appendiculate, almost as long as the petals, glandular outside, tomentose within; *petals* 5, large for a small plant, whitish outside, clear purple within. *Heps* pyriform, somewhat bristly, reddish or orange, long persistent in winter.

This grows spontaneously all over Germany where it is known as the 'Rose of Austria'. It is the type of the *gallica* group of our gardens, yet scarcely known in France. Du Pont's specimen passed with his collection to Luxembourg, but this year we have rediscovered it in Le Dru's collection and it is from there that our model comes. Cultivation in France seems to have increased its overall size compared with wild specimens received direct from Germany. Rau cites a remarkable variety *R. pumila hispida* with bristly stems and sepals much longer than the petals which are a deeper purple colour. The roots of *R. pumila*, like those of *Rubus caesius*, rapidly extend far and wide, especially in arable land where the resulting suckers impede harvesting of crops and defy efforts at eradication.

Rosa Pumila.   *Rosier d'Amour.*

P. J. Redouté pinx.   Imprimerie de Rémond.   Bessin sculp.

ROSA CENTIFOLIA CRENATA
'CRENATE-LEAVED CABBAGE ROSE'

Moderately tufted *shrub* about 0.6 m tall; *branches* numerous, glandular hispid, with small, almost straight *prickles* which drop readily so that adult branches are unarmed. *Leaflets* 3–5, rotund or subrotund, cordate at the base, deeply crenate, each lobe tipped by a glandular mucro and denticulate on the margins, upperside dark green, underside paler; petioles tomentose, unarmed. *Flowers* 1–3 at the branch tips, like those of the common Cabbage Rose but smaller and less fragrant; pedicels covered in sticky scented glandular hairs; *receptacles* ovoid, rather short, bristly as are the *sepals; petals* numerous, those at the centre rather curled and crumpled.

Said to have been raised from seed by Du Pont, who distributed it, the 'Crenate-leaved Rose' is sought after for its odd foliage, and blooms but rarely on its own roots. Grafted plants flower freely if unpruned. It is rather scarce in collections. A modification with rather more elongated leaflets is in cultivation under the name 'Oak-leaved Rose'.

Rosa Centifolia crenata.   *Rosier Centfeuilles à folioles crenelées.*

P. J. Redouté pinx.   Imprimerie de Rémond   Chapuy sculp.

ROSA MULTIFLORA CARNEA
'FLESH-PINK MULTIFLORA'

Branches long and climbing, straight, glabrous, reddish; *prickles* often geminate and infrastipular or more or less scattered. *Leaflets* 5 or 7, rather small, ovate to elongated ovate, almost sessile, soft to the touch, simply dentate, upperside green and glabrous, underside paler and pubescent; petioles villous with small hooked prickles; stipules pectinately pinnatifid. *Flowers* numerous, in dense broad panicles borne on the laterals, small, almost full, faintly scented; bracts incised on both margins like the stipules; peduncles and pedicels villous like the petioles; *receptacles* ovoid to subglobose, pubescent; *sepals* 3 pinnatifid, 2 simple, acute, shorter than the petals, pubescent; *petals* many-seriate, pale pink; *styles* free, villous, the ones at the centre fasciculate, outer ones divergent.

This native of China was introduced to England by T. Evans around 1804, where it flowered for the first time in Colville's nursery. Boursault brought it from London to Paris in 1808 where it flowered in August 1812 in Dr. Cartier's garden.

The long branches of *multiflora* lend themselves to many uses: draping arbours and bowers, entwined into garlands or pyramids, and by means of support on trellises for covering walls to a great height. Grafted plants succeed the best. In the open air winter frosts destroy *multiflora* in the Paris area unless it is covered for protection.

Rosa Multiflora carnea.   *Rosier Multiflore à fleurs carnées.*

P. J. Redouté pinx.   Imprimerie de Rémond   Talbeaux sculp.

ROSA MULTIFLORA PLATYPHYLLA
'BIG-LEAVED MULTIFLORA'

Branches tall, as in *R. multiflora rosea* but more robust. *Leaflets* more rounded and 3–4 times larger than those of the species. *Flowers* also much larger though perhaps less numerous, an attractive shade of purple. This magnificent rose, remarkable for its foliage and petal colour, was introduced by Noisette for whom it flowered in September 1819. He had found it in 1817 in a market garden near London, where it had come as seed from Japan. So far it has been grown only in a peaty soil in a temperate house, but there is every likelihood of its being acclimatised outdoors.

Rosa multiflora gets its name from the abundance of blooms it produces. The panicle of 60–100 flowers, pectinate stipules and bracts, and sarmentose branches easily distinguish it from all others, especially *R. moschata* which is close, but further differs in its coherent styles and disposition of flowers. All the varieties reproduce with the greatest ease from cuttings and layers, and *multiflora* can be successfully grafted on the wild briar. If buds are inserted on a solitary stem 2.4–3 m high, the effect will be picturesque, like that of a weeping willow. To avoid frost damage, pruning should be postponed until the end of April. Inflorescences scarcely ever flower twice, so sterile shoots should be pruned less severely to encourage new growth and flowers.

Rosa Multiflora platyphylla.   *Rosier Multiflore à grandes feuilles.*

P.J. Redouté pinx.   Imprimerie de Remond   Langlois sculp.

ROSA VILLOSA TEREBENTHINA
Lit. 'TURPENTINE-SCENTED DOWNY ROSE'

Tufted *shrub* 1.2–1.5 m high; *branches* glabrous; *prickles* yellowish, almost straight, sparse on adult branches, geminate on young branches and inflorescences. *Leaflets* 5 or 7, very large, subovate, deeply and unequally dentate, covered all over in sticky glandular hairs and turpentine-scented when bruised; upperside dark green, underside glaucous; petioles villous, with small, recurved, yellowish prickles; stipules dilated, decurrent, denticulate, glandular, villous. *Flowers* 1–4, subumbellate, lateral and terminal, small, almost scentless; pedicels short, glandular hispid; bracts acute, broad-based; *receptacles* subglobose, hispid; *sepals* acute, simple or pinnate; *petals* 5, red fading to whitish at the base, irregularly notched, often mucronate; *styles* little exserted, with stigmas in a roundish head.

Rosa Villosa Terebenthina

Rosier Velu à odeur de Térébenthine

P. Redouté pinx.

Imprimerie de Remond.

Bessin sculp.

ROSA PARVIFLORA FLORE MULTIPLICI
'SMALL-FLOWERED ROSE'

Tufted *bush* 0.6 m or more in height; *branches* weak, glabrous; *prickles* infrastipular, long, needle-like, almost straight, opposite as well as many more scattered along the branches. *Leaflets* 5, ovate, acute at both ends, upperside green, at most slightly glossy, underside paler; petioles pubescent on the upperside, with small prickles on the underside; stipules narrow, decurrent, denticulate. *Flowers* 2(-3) at the tips of the laterals; pedicels glandular hispid; receptacles subcompressed globose; *sepals* long, similarly glandular; *petals* many-seriate, bright pink, paler at the centre.

This small shrub originates in North America and is variously known in nurseries as the 'Carolina Rose', 'Virginia Rose' and 'Double Pennsylvanian Rose'. It is a double-flowered derivative of Bosc's *Rosa carolina* from which it differs only by the slightly flattened receptacles and the slightly villous petioles. These differences are so slight that we unite *R. parviflora* under *R. carolina* together with many other North American roses, although seed-raising from these "species" has produced so many intermediates that we are not yet in a position to sort out species, varieties and subvarieties.

Rosa parviflora is closely related to Willdenow's *R. gemella*, but in that the prickles are not infrastipular but infra-axillary, the leaflets are longer and their ribs pubescent. This rose suckers freely, the old canes dying out, so that if suckers are wholly pruned away it is lost to gardens. To keep it going one should transplant suckers regularly.

Remarkable for the size of its leaflets and their resinous odour, this rose is not yet common, but should be fit to decorate English parks and gardens. It is confused with the 'Red Nutmeg Rose' (*R. evratina*), which differs in leaflets and other characteristics. We regard *evratina* as an anomalous descendant of *R. alba* and *R. villosa*. It is reputedly a native of North America, although not mentioned by Nuttall, and it succeeds only in shade and beneath large trees, being less vigorous when exposed to sun.

Rosa parvi-flora.   *Rosier à petites fleurs.*

P. J. Redouté pinx.   Imprimerie de Rémond.   Langlois sculp.

ROSA RUBIGINOSA FLORE SEMI-PLENO
'SEMI-DOUBLE SWEETBRIAR'

0.9–1.2 m high; *stems* glabrous, branched; *prickles* sparse, recurved, some long, some short. *Leaflets* 5(–7), medium-sized, subrotund, upperside almost glabrous, underside and margins covered with sticky, glandular, rust-coloured hairs giving an apple scent when rubbed; petioles villous, prickly; stipules fairly broad, glandular as are all foliaceous parts. *Flowers* 1–4; pedicels and ovoid *receptacles* glandular hispid; *sepals* pinnatifid, glandular outside, whitish woolly within; *petals* 10–15(–20), notched, pale pink whitening towards the base. *Heps* orange-red, subglabrous at maturity, long persistent.

This, the 'Little Hessian' of nurseries, was introduced by Redouté who raised it from seed 15 years ago and distributed it via nurseries throughout France and abroad. A derivative is known with much broader and more rounded leaves and subumbellate inflorescences – probably a semi-double modification of *R. rubiginosa canadensis* Poiret. Le Jeune claims to have raised a typical *rubiginosa* from a seed of *R. centifolia*.

Rosa Rubiginosa flore semi-pleno.   *Rosier Rouillé a fleurs semi-doubles.*

P. J. Redouté pinx.   Imprimerie de Remond.   Chapuy sculp.

ROSA NOISETTIANA [Thory hybr. n.]
'PHILIPPE NOISETTE ROSE'

Superb *shrub* 2.4–3 m high; *branches* glabrous; *prickles* fairly strong,
a little hooked, reddish on the flowering branches, brown on the
adult stems. *Leaflets* 5–7, acute ovate, rarely obtuse, simply and
finely crenulate, glabrous, upperside green, underside paler;
petioles villous, with many small recurved prickles sometimes
extending up to the midrib of the odd leaflet; stipules acute, denticulate, gland-edged. *Flowers* lateral and terminal, (1–)3–6, often
grouped in panicles of up to 130, opening successively, the first out
being larger than those of the 'Musk Rose', the others about the
same size, very sweetly scented; peduncles, elongated pedicels
and ovoid *receptacles* shortly and densely woolly; *sepals* 2 entire, 3
pinnate, acute, woolly within, gland-edged; *petals* 7–8-seriate,
white flushed pink, a little yellowish towards the base, irregularly
notched; *styles* free; *stigmas* a little reddish.

This was produced by Philippe Noisette, one of the most skilful
North American nurserymen, and propagated in France by his
brother Louis Noisette. Our specimen came from his choice collection where it bloomed in 1818. We consider it a hybrid of *R.
moschata* and *R. chinensis*, with which it shares the foliage, flower
disposition and season. However, the former is distinguished by
its coherent styles and smaller, pure white flowers; the latter by its
reflexed sepals, long tortuous stamens bent inwards over the styles,
and continuous flowering. Seed raising may show us if it will breed
true and· constitute a new species.

It blooms abundantly from July up to the frosts and a young
specimen was frost hardy in 1820, although we took the precaution
of covering it with leaves. When acclimatised it will be an ornament to our gardens, above all for the perfume which is as good
as that of *centifolia* although different.

Rosa Noisettiana.

Rosier de Philippe Noisette.

P. Redouté pinx.   Imprimerie de Remond.   Langlois sculp.

ROSA INDICA SUBALBA
'WHITE CHINA ROSE'

Shrub about 0.5 m tall; upper *branches* generally glabrous but lower ones armed with sparse, somewhat recurved *prickles*. *Leaflets* 3–5 (–7), ovate, acute at both ends, upperside green and glabrous, underside paler; petioles with small, hooked, yellowish prickles; stipules long, narrow, very acute, finely denticulate. *Flowers* 1–4, lateral and terminal, sometimes subumbellate; *receptacles* elongated ovoid, glabrous as are the long pedicels; bracts very small, ovate, acute; *sepals* entire or rarely with 1–2 minute simple pinnules; *petals* 3–6-seriate, irregularly notched, very pale pink at first, later almost pure white, sometimes ending up with small reddish spots; *stamens* and *styles* as in the China Roses.

Obtained from seed by Cels in 1804, this was then known as 'Cels's China', but was later renamed to avoid confusion with 'Cels's Rose'. It is a weak and tender plant, and the frosts of January 1820 killed off most in the neighbourhood of Paris. Pot plants sheltered in the orangery in winter fared better; in the open air it should be cut to within 2.5 cm of the roots. It should be lifted every two years and replanted in a mixture of loam and humus, or better kept in a bed of peat; but it is best to use pots which can be brought inside in winter.

Rosa Indica subalba.

Rosier du Bengale à fleurs blanches.

P. J. Redouté pinx.

Imprimerie de Remond.

Lemaire sculp.

ROSA NIVEA
'SNOW-WHITE ROSE'
[Contributed by De Candolle]

Rootstock suckering somewhat; *stems* suberect, loosely tufted, branched, unarmed, 0.6–3(–4.5) m tall; *branches* numerous, glabrous; *prickles* few, sparse, greyish, compressed and dilated lengthwise at the base, thin, hooked. *Leaflets* 3(–5), lanceolate ovate, simply serrate, quite glabrous, glossy, bright green; stipules narrow, sublinear, serrate, slightly glandular; petioles with 1–4 short, almost straight prickles. *Flowers* lateral or rarely terminal, solitary, quite single, 7.5 cm in diameter, scentless; ovoid *receptacles* and upper part of pedicels glandular hispid; *sepals* lanceolate, linear, glabrous, quite entire; *petals* rounded, very open, snow white, subcrenate; *stamens* about 100; *styles* slender, villous, coherent; *stigmas* in a compact hemispherical head.

This rose is probably native to China and was introduced to Europe by Lord Macartney. (Thory considers it to be native to New Georgia in America, collected by Michaux and the same as *R. laevigata* of the Royal Garden.) It is hardy at Montpellier and flowers in late May, before *R. bracteata*. It can be grafted on the dog rose but does better on its own roots, the suckers being a means of propagation. It appreciates a porous but moist soil, its foliage yellowing with too much or too little moisture. A double variant, if obtainable, would be one of the most beautiful roses by virtue of the brilliant whiteness of the flowers and the beauty of the foliage.

Dumont de Courset seems to have confused this species with *R. bracteata*. *R. nivea* differs by the 3(–5) leaflets, glabrous branches, pedicels and rounded entire petals. Equated with *R. sinica* L. by some, it differs by its globose, glabrous receptacle and differently shaped sepals. *Rosa trifoliata* is inapplicable as a name here as there are sometimes 4 or 5 leaflets.

Rosa Nivea.

Rosier blanc de Neige.

P. J. Redouté pinx.   Imprimerie de Rémond   Langlois sculp.

ROSA GEMINATA
'TWIN-FLOWERED ROSE'

Habit like the 'Van Eeden Rose'; *branches* at first suberect, later prostrate like those of *arvensis* but not rooting; *prickles* sparse, of unequal size, some straight, others recurved. *Leaflets* 3, 5 or 7, rounded ovate, generally simply dentate, the teeth sometimes glandular, upperside glabrous, underside pubescent; petioles villous, with glands and small recurved prickles; stipules lanceolate, acute, denticulate, gland-edged. *Flowers* (1–)2–3 at the branch tips, lateral or terminal; pedicels long, stiff, close together, glandular hispid; *receptacles* abruptly rounded at the base or fusiform (midway between *alba* and *damascena*), the base with hairs and sessile glands; *sepals* appendiculate, covered in purplish, stalked glands; *petals* 5, large, satiny white flushed pink at the apex, cordately notched, very soft, a little crumpled like those of a poppy; bud white, sometimes pink-tipped before opening; *styles* as long as the stamens, distinct, villous at the base. *Heps* small in relation to the size of the corolla, broad based and tapering above.

The 'Twin-flowered Rose' grows in ploughed soil along with *R. pumila* in Germany, where it was found and sent to us by Rau. Among single roses it qualifies as one of the best of the genus. The receptacle varies and is sometimes glandular hispid all over. We had previously referred it to *Rosa alba*, as shown by the form of the receptacle and hep, and the subrotund, dentate leaflets with upperside glabrous and underside villous. Rau, however, contests this and regards his *geminata* as a distinct species.

Rosa geminata   *Rosier à fleurs géminées.*

P. J. Redouté pinx.   Imprimerie de Remond   Chapuy sculp.

ROSA DUMETORUM
'THICKET ROSE'

Bush 0.9–1.8 m high; *branches* quite glabrous; *prickles* hooked, some scattered but most paired near the stipules. *Leaflets* 5 (–7), rounded ovate, simply dentate but upper teeth sometimes unequal, rather firm to the touch, veins prominent and almost parallel, upperside green and glabrous, underside paler and tomentose; petioles prickly; stipules quite entire, villous, acute, denticulate. *Flowers* small for the size of the shrub, 3–5 on the laterals, in a short, compact corymb; pedicels and *receptacles* glabrous; *sepals* pinnatifid; *petals* 5, very pale pink, cordately notched. *Heps* globose, bright red.

Native to North Europe and common enough in woods and hedges around Paris, this rose varies in habit according to the environment. The leaflets are sometimes tiny or average, as in the plant figured, sometimes very large or elongated and pointed. In many specimens the prickles are little or not enlarged at the base (*R. dumetorum litigiosa* D.C.). We consider *dumetorum* inseparable from *R. collina* D.C. non Jacq. on account of the leaves being constantly villous below.

Rosa Dumetorum.   *Rosier des Buissons*

P. J. Redouté pinx.   Imprimerie de Remond.   Chapuy sculp.

ROSA TOMENTOSA FLORE MULTIPLICI
'DOUBLE DOWNY ROSE'

Bush 1.2–1.5 m tall; *prickles* stout, greyish, almost straight, dilated at the base, sparse, sometimes paired near the stipules. *Leaflets* 5(–7), large, villous on both surfaces, bidentate; petioles villous, with small hooked prickles; stipules broad, denticulate, acute, sometimes leafy-tipped. *Flowers* (1–)3 at the branch tips; pedicels densely glandular hispid; *receptacles* ovoid, likewise hispid; bracts 2, acute ovate, somewhat leafy-tipped; *petals* 4–5-seriate, pale pink, well-formed, irregularly notched, yellowish towards the base; *sepals* elongated, often entire, sometimes simply pinnulate, downy within, glandular outside. *Heps* large, a little swollen midway, red, finally unarmed.

This is a member of the Rosae Villosae having the leaves villous on both sides. It is fairly common in gardens and is often confused with the double *R. villosa*, but that has more slender and much loftier stems, globose receptacles and darker pink blooms. It probably arose as a seedling of the wild *R. tomentosa*, and not only are the flowers bulkier from extra petals, but the foliage is also larger. Grown in shade in a cool site it produces a multitude of blooms in early summer, faintly scented but very satisfying. Rau claims to see the prototype of all Villosae in *R. rubiginosa*, the Rubiginosae differing only in their smaller size factor from the Villosae.

Rosa Tomentosa.

Rosier Cotonneux.

P. J. Redouté pinx.

Imprimerie de Rémond.

Bessin sculp.

ROSA MOLLISSIMA FLORE SUBMULTIPLICI
'DOUBLE SOFT-LEAVED ROSE'

About 1.2 m tall; *prickles* sparse, almost straight, rather like those of *R. villosa*. *Leaflets* 7, rounded ovate, villous, so soft as to feel like fine cloth to the touch; petioles villous, with minute recurved prickles. *Flowers* 2–3, lateral and terminal on the branch tips; pedicels glandular hispid; *receptacles* subglobose, glabrous or sometimes more or less hispid; *sepals* spatulate, pinnatifid, sometimes leafy-tipped, villous and soft like the leaves; *petals* 4-seriate, a unique shade of carmine suffused with white. *Heps* oblong, glabrous or rarely also hispid.

A member of the Villosae, this is distinct from *R. villosa* only by the typically smooth receptacle and type of indumentum. Willdenow first considered it a species, but later made it a variety of *villosa*. It will always be in demand in ornamental gardens for the beautiful and singular colour of the flowers. It blooms in early spring and relishes exposure to sun. Pruning should be avoided except to remove dead wood.

Rosa mollissima.

Rosier à feuilles molles.

P. J. Redouté pinx.   Imprimerie de Remond   Victor s.

ROSA GALLICA CAERULEA
'BLUISH-LEAVED PROVINS ROSE'

Bush about 0.6 m tall; *prickles* unequal, reddish, almost straight. *Leaflets* 7, oblong, acute, firm to the touch, denticulate, glaucous green with a bluish tinge; petioles slightly villous and glandular, with small yellowish prickles; stipules gland-edged. *Flowers* 1–3 at the branch tips; pedicels and subovoid *receptacles* covered in small sessile glands; *sepals* 3 pinnatifid and 2 simple, downy within, glandular outside; *petals* 7–8-seriate, clear red variegated with numerous closely packed spots of a darker hue. Otherwise similar to the gallicas.

Redouté raised this rose from seed himself in his garden at Fleury. It is notable for its almost blue foliage. It is rarely seen on its own roots, but fine grafted specimens are in Boursault's collection in Paris, and in the Royal Garden at Sèvres, although overall it is not common. It needs the same cultivation as the Provins Roses but likes exposure to sun which enhances the blue colour of the leaves.

Rosa Gallica cuerulea.   *Rosier de Provins a feuilles bleuâtres.*

P.J. Redouté pinx.   Imprimerie de Remond   Eug. Talbaux sculp.

ROSA INERMIS [Thory sp. n.]
'ROSE WITHOUT A THORN'

Very tufed *bush* 1.2–1.5 m tall; *branches* smooth, greenish, quite unarmed. *Leaves* medium-sized; *leaflets* 7–9, elliptic, unequally dentate, upperside green, underside paler, glabrous on both surfaces; petioles roughish to the touch from small prickles; stipules a little dentate, gland-edged, dilated, not replicate as in *R. hudsoniana* with which it might be confused. *Flowers* almost always solitary at the ends of the laterals, 5–6 cm in diameter; pedicels elongated, glandular hispid; *receptacles* turbinate, similarly hispid at the base only; *sepals* 3 pinnatifid, 2 simple, longer than the petals in an open flower, ciliate, downy within; *petals* 7–8-seriate, delicate pink, faintly scented; *styles* free; *stigmas* distinct.

A common rose in our gardens, this is one of the first to bloom. Du Pont was persuaded that it came from the Far East and called it *Rosa chinensis*, but it hails from the Swiss Alps and we recognise it as *R. turbinata* Villars, *R. alpina multiplex* Degrasse and *R. alpina turbinata* Desvaux. Delaunay called it *Rosa inermis* and it is one of the Group Turbinatae. It flowers at the start of May and is undemanding, all soils suiting it. It should only be grown on its own roots, since if grafted it is inferior and the later flowers abort.

Rosa Inermis.

Rosier Turbiné sans épines.

P. J. Redouté pinx.

Imprimerie de Rémond

Lemaire sculp.

ROSA CAMPANULATA FLORE ALBO
'WHITE BELL ROSE'

Bush about 0.6 m high; *prickles* almost straight on the inflorescences, a little curved on the main axis. *Leaflets* 7 or 9, glabrous, ovate, simply dentate, upperside glaucous green, underside paler; petioles slightly villous, with minute yellowish prickles; stipules narrow, acute. *Flowers* 1–3 at the branch tips, slightly scented; pedicels long, glandular hispid; *receptacles* pointed below and flared above, almost campanulate, hispid towards the base; *sepals* entire or pinnulate, densely downy within, gland-edged outside; *petals* 2–2.5 cm across, 5–6-seriate, white, those at the centre flushed pink, yellowing towards the base, irregularly notched; *stamens* numerous.

This differs from the 'Frankfort Rose' by the white flowers and prickly inflorescences; from *R. rapa* Bosc by the glossy leaves; from *R. turbinata inermis* by the completely glabrous leaflets and from *R. rosenbergiana* by the hispid branches. Above all, the receptacle shape and abortion of many flowers align it naturally with the Group Turbinatae. It was obtained from seed by Cugnot, a Parisian gardener, and is to be found grafted in many gardens. It is a fine rose, and the only member of Turbinatae with white blooms.

Rosa Campanulata alba.   *Rosier Campanulé à fleurs blanches.*

P. J. Redouté pinx.   Imprimerie de Rémond   Langlois sculp.

ROSA RUBIGINOSA ACULEATISSIMA [Thory var. n.]
'PRICKLY SWEETBRIAR'

Tufted *bush* 1.2 m high or more; *branches* bristly with a large number of stout, unequal, mostly almost straight, densely packed prickles. *Leaflets* 7 (–9), somewhat viscous, rounded ovate, glandular biserrate, upperside slightly pubescent; petioles pubescent, glandular, with small hooked prickles; stipules entire, gland-edged. *Flowers* fairly small, (1–)3 at the branch tips; pedicels and ovoid *receptacles* glandular hispid; *sepals* pinnatifid, spatulate; *petals* 5, pale pink, faintly yellow towards the base; *styles* villous, very short.

This variety is of interest only to collectors and offers little by way of garden ornament. Du Pont raised it from seed and distributed it around 1810. It is much like *R. rubiginosa triflora* Rau, differing only by the denser armature. It likes full sun and flowers for more than a month, especially if unpruned and left to itself.

Rosa rubiginosa aculeatissima.   *Rosier rouillé très epineux.*

P. J. Redouté pinx.   Imprimerie de Remond.   Chapuy sculp.

ROSA PIMPINELLIFOLIA FLORE ALBO SUBMULTIPLICI
'DOUBLE WHITE BURNET ROSE'

Branching *bush* about 75 cm high; *prickles* very numerous, unequal, some straight, some recurved. *Leaflets* 5, 7 or 9, round or rounded ovate, deeply dentate, upperside bright green, underside paler and sometimes reddish; petioles glabrous or more often with small yellowish hooked prickles; stipules fairly broad, denticulate. *Flowers* solitary at the ends of the laterals; pedicels broadening above and narrowing below, glandular hispid; *receptacles* sub-globose, quite glabrous, in part flushed reddish brown; *sepals* entire, acute, glabrous outside, downy within; *petals* 8–10-seriate, white, some pointed, others cordately notched. *Heps* globose, bright red maturing to black.

It is to Descemet that amateurs owe this rose with its remarkable elegance and beautiful blooms. For long rare and expensive, it is today stocked by almost all nurseries under the name 'White Pompon'. It makes a fine display grafted rather low down on *canina*, when it will grow vigorously and produce magnificent heads in the second year. For the fullest blooms in maximum number, it needs a site facing East and especially no pruning except for dead wood. Additional flowers in the autumn are not unknown.

Rosa Pimpinellifolia alba
flore multiplei.

Rosier Pimprenelle blanc
à fleurs doubles.

P. J. Redouté pinx. Imprimerie de Rémond Teillard sculp.

ROSA CENTIFOLIA ANGLICA RUBRA
'CUMBERLAND ROSE'

Bush about 0.6 m tall; *prickles* numerous, unequal, almost straight. *Leaflets* (3–)5, broad, soft to the touch, bidentate, margins whitish woolly and glandular hispid, upperside green, underside paler and pubescent; petioles villous, unarmed. *Flowers* strongly perfumed, 3–4 at the branch tips; pedicels elongated, lax, glandular hispid; *receptacles* thick, ovoid, also glandular hispid; *sepals* 3 pinnatifid, 2 simple, glandular outside, whitish downy within; *corolla* large, to 7.5 cm across; *petals* 10–12-seriate, all bright pink.

This magnificent cultivar, notable for the rounded form of the bloom, is highly esteemed in England where it has been known for a long time although grown in France for only 15–20 years. It differs from common *centifolia* only in the uniform colour of the flowers, those of *centifolia* being darker towards the centre. We have seen superb grafted specimens at Catel's garden in Paris, and many nurseries stock it. It is delicate and requires an easterly exposure. We also grow a modification with mossy sepals and receptacles, which we propose to publish.

Rosa centifolia Anglica rubra.　　　*Rosier de Cumberland.*

P.J. Redouté pinx.　　　Imprimerie de Remond.　　　Langlois sculp.

ROSA PIMPINELLIFOLIA MAJOR FLORE VARIEGATO
Lit. 'HUNDRED-CROWNS BURNET ROSE'

Rather tufted *bush* about 0.6 m high; *branches* brown; *prickles* very numerous, dense, fine, unequal, almost straight. *Leaflets* 7–9(–11), obtuse ovate, simply dentate, quite entire at the base, glabrous all over; petioles glabrous; stipules acute. *Flowers* faintly scented, 1 (–2) at the tips of the laterals; pedicels and *receptacles* glabrous or hispid; *sepals* simple, acute or spatulate; *petals* 5, fairly large, attractively and irregularly variegated, greyish white, pale pink or dark pink, yellow towards the base, cordately notched. *Heps* small, red at first, black at maturity.

Vibert introduced this rose under the name 'Pimprenelle Belle Laure' No 2. Descemet had obtained it as a seedling of a much smaller rose of Du Pont's which died out in 1819, surviving as only a single bush with Le Meunier. The flower is finer and has more vivid variegation. It blooms in May and seems hardier than its parent. It is rare in gardens, although available from Vibert.

Rosa Pimpinellifolia flore variegato.   *La Pimprenelle aux Cent-Ecus.*

P. J. Redouté pinx.   Imprimerie de Rémond.   Langlois sculp.

ROSA GALLICA GRANATI
'POMEGRANATE-FRUITED PROVINS ROSE'

Tufted *bush* about 75 cm tall; *prickles* numerous, unequal, some straight, others recurved. *Leaflets* 5(–7), large, finely bidentate, overall a little less thick and rugose than in other gallicas, upperside pale green, underside and margins tomentose; petioles villous, with small prickles; stipules fairly large, denticulate. *Flowers* in late June, almost scentless, 3–4 the branch tips; pedicels and rounded *receptacles* with small glandular hairs; *sepals* elongated, sometimes leafy, 3 pinnatifid and 2 simple, glandular outside and villous within; *petals* 4–5-seriate, rather pallid pink, almost like those of the common *centifolia; styles* somewhat elongated and subfasciculate.

This rose is outstanding for the flower colour and fruit shape, which distantly resembles that of a pomegranate. It was obtained from seed by Vilmorin some years ago, and although it is now in a few amateur collections it is not widespread. Its cultivation is the same as for the gallicas and it should be pruned back hard.

Rosa Gallica Granatus.   *Rosier de France a Pomme de Grenade.*

P. J. Redouté pinx.   Imprimerie de Remond   Victor sculp.

ROSA SEPIUM FLORE SUBMULTIPLICI
'SEMI-DOUBLE HEDGE ROSE'

Branching *shrub* 1.2–1.5 m tall; *prickles* fairly numerous, recurved, somewhat whitish. *Leaflets* 5 or 7, small, a little less distantly spaced than in the type, acute at both ends, glandular serrate, upperside smooth, underside glandular; petioles also glandular, with small prickles; stipules denticulate. *Flowers* 1–4; pedicels and ovoid *receptacles* glabrous; *sepals* 3 [Misprinted "2"] pinnatifid, 2 simple, whitish downy within; *petals* 4–5-seriate, pale red, white towards the base, cordately notched; *styles* almost glabrous, subfasciculate.

This rose flowered for the first time last summer for Cugnot who obtained it from seed. Its blooms are elegant and appear at the beginning of June. It is very robust and needs no special care – any soil or exposure suits it, and it should not be pruned.

Rosa sepium flore submultiplici.

Rosier des hayes a fleurs semi doubles.

P. J. Redouté pinx.   Imprimerie de Remond.   Eug. Talbeaux sculp

ROSA HUDSONIANA SCANDENS
'CLIMBING HUDSON'S ROSE'

Tall-climbing *shrub* suitable for covering arbours and bowers; *branches* smooth, unarmed, reddish brown where exposed to the sun. *Leaflets* 7, elongated but broader than in *R. hudsoniana salicifolia*, glabrous on both surfaces, distant, simply dentate, upperside bright green, underside paler; petioles with small, hooked, reddish prickles on the underside; stipules replicate, acute, slightly downy along the edges. *Flowers* 1 (–2) on the laterals, in May; pedicels and ovoid *receptacles* glabrous; *sepals* glabrous outside, slightly downy within; *petals* 3–4-seriate, pale pink. *Heps* not seen.

Lindley cites *R. hudsoniana* in the synonymy of *R. carolina*, but it is unarmed and has a glabrous or very rarely hairy receptacle whereas *carolina* has long, almost straight prickles, including infrastipular pairs, and an indumentum on the receptacle.

Rosa Hudsoniana scandens.

Rosier d'Hudson à tiges grimpantes.

P. J. Redouté pinx.

Imprimerie de Remond.

Tillard sculp.

ROSA ALPINA VULGARIS
'COMMON ALPINE ROSE'

Shrub 0.9–1.2 m tall; *stems* long, diffuse, in general glabrous, sometimes aciculate at the base. *Leaflets* 7–9(–11), rather small, obtuse ovate, biserrate, upperside bright green, underside paler; petioles a little rough to the touch; stipules dilated, denticulate. *Flowers* 1–3 at the tips of the laterals; pedicels and *receptacles* hispid in the plant figured but often one or the other is glabrous; *sepals* entire, acuminate or sometimes spatulate; *petals* 5, bright red, a little yellowed towards the base, cordately notched; *stigmas* amassed in a compact head. *Heps* red, ovoid, glabrous or thinly hispid in some varieties.

This rose, one of the first to bloom in the Paris area, is common in the Alps, Vosges, Pyrenees and mountains of Auvergne and elsewhere, where it blooms from May to the end of July. It has sported many varieties which have been unjustifiably raised to specific status: *R. pyrenaica* Gouan, *R. hispida* Kroch, *R. hybrida* Villars, *R. lagenaria* Villars, *R. pendulina* L., *R. sanguisorbaefolia* Dillenius, etc.

Rosa Alpina vulgaris.   *Rosier des Alpes commun.*

P. J. Redouté pinx.   Imprimerie de Rémond.   Chapuy sculp.

ROSA ROSENBERGIANA
'ROSENBERG'S ROSE'

Very tufted *bush* 0.75–1 m high; *prickles* very numerous, yellowish, almost straight, of unequal lengths. *Leaflets* 5(–7), ovate, deeply crenate, upperside glabrous, underside tomentose; petioles villous, with small prickles; stipules entire. *Flowers* subumbellate at the branch tips; pedicels and turbinate *receptacles* bristly from a large number of small unequal prickles similar to those on the branches; *sepals* aciculate outside, entire, acute or more often spatulate or even leafy; *petals* many-seriate, white, flushed pink towards the centre. *Heps* not seen.

This rose, a member of the Turbinatae, produces a large number of buds in June which abort and only rarely open, whence the name 'Black Nutmeg Rose'. It is dedicated to the memory of Jean-Charles Rosenberg, author of the Rhodologie, an early monograph of the rose from the start of the seventeenth century. Although the descriptions of species are only copies from Bauhin, he adds critical comments and common names, and his work served as a model for later rose monographs.

Rosa Rosenberguana.   *Rosier de Rosenberg*

P. J. Redouté pinx.   Imprimerie de Remond.   Langlois sculp.

ROSA CENTIFOLIA ANEMONOIDES
'HUNDRED-PETALLED ANEMONE ROSE'

Somewhat tufted *bush* about 0.6 m high; stems aciculate and glandular hispid. *Leaflets* 5 (–7), elliptic ovate, deeply crenate, soft to the touch, margins lightly downy and glandular, upperside green, underside pubescent; petioles villous, rather rough although without obvious prickles; stipules acute. *Flowers* 2–3 at the branch tips; long pedicels and ovoid *receptacles* densely glandular hispid; *sepals* 3 pinnatifid and 2 simple, glandular outside, whitish woolly within; *petals* 5–6-seriate, pink, the innermost shorter, replicate, concave and resembling the flower of an anemone.

The nurseryman Poilpré found this rose in a garden near Le Mans about 10 years ago and distributed it under the name 'Anemone Rose' as given it by Tascher. It can be propagated only by grafting or layering and is very delicate, succeeding only in a sheltered site and bearing few flowers. Like all centifolias it should be pruned hard in February. It is not yet widely distributed, but Noisette and Poilpré both stock it. It should be grafted often to ensure its preservation.

Rosa Centifolia Anemonoides.   *La Centfeuilles Anemone.*

P. J. Redouté pinx.   Imprimerie de Remond   Victor sculp.

ROSA HUDSONIANA SUBCORYMBOSA
'SUBCORYMBOSE HUDSON ROSE'

Height 0.6–0.9 m; *branches* diffuse, reddish, particularly where exposed to the sun, quite unarmed. *Leaflets* 5, 7 or 9, elongated elliptic, acute at both ends, glabrous on both surfaces, simply serrulate, upperside green, underside glaucous; petioles slightly villous, sometimes with small prickles; stipules narrow, replicate. *Flowers* subcorymbose at the branch tips; pedicels with a few glandular hairs; *receptacles* elongated ovoid, glabrous or bristly on the one plant; *sepals* simple, acute or spatulate, glandular outside and on the edges, whitish downy within; *petals* 5–6-seriate, soft pink, irregularly rounded at the tip; *stamens* very numerous; *stigmas* amassed in a sessile head.

This variant of 'Hudson's Rose' differs from that with willow leaves (Vol. I p. 74) by the less elongated, elliptic leaves, the more constantly glandular receptacles and the semi-double blooms. *R. hudsoniana scandens* is easily distinguished from the other two by its climbing habit and flowers most often solitary. The specimen illustrated came from Ternaux at Autueil, who obtained it recently from seed.

Rosa hudsoniana Subcorymbosa.   *Rosier d'hudson a fleurs presqu en Corymbe.*

P.J. Redoute pinx.   Imprimerie de Remond.   Eug. Talbaux sculp.

ROSA INDICA SUBVIOLACEA
'NEAR-VIOLET CHINA ROSE'

Prickles stout, short, hooked, much dilated at the base. *Leaflets* 5 or 7, acute, crenate, purplish edged, upperside green, underside paler; petioles slightly tomentose, with small, yellowish, very sharp prickles; stipules decurrent, acute, denticulate. *Flowers* the size of those of common *multiflora*, subumbellate at the branch tips; pedicels slender, with glandular hairs; bracts basal, opposite, long, simple or sometimes leafy; *receptacles* small, ovoid, glabrous; *sepals* glabrous, recurved before anthesis as in all China roses; *corolla* almost full, of a beautiful crimson shading towards violet – a unique feature distinguishing this from all others.

A derivative of the 'Crimson China Rose' (Vol. 1 p. 30), this was obtained from seed in Ternaux's garden and is distributed under the name he gave it. Today it is available from many nurseries. Collectors of China roses will be eager to have it, not only for the fine colour of the petals, but also because it blooms continuously – in summer in beds in the garden, in winter in frames where it is sheltered.

Rosa Indica subviolacea.   *Rosier des Indes a fleurs presque violettes.*

P.J. Redouté pinx.   Imprimerie de Remond   Langlois sculp.

ROSA GALLICA PONTIANA
'ANDRÉ DU PONT'S ROSE'

Bush 0.9–1.2 m high; *stems* dark green; *branches* diffuse, numerous; *prickles* short, unequal, dense. *Leaflets* 5 or 7, ovate or round, firm and brittle, bidenticulate, gland-edged, upperside glabrous, underside villous; petioles villous, with a few small prickles; stipules enlarged, denticulate. *Flowers* clustered at the branch tips; pedicels long, more or less hispid; *receptacles* globose or elongated ovoid, glandular hispid as are the pinnatifid *sepals; corolla* large; *petals* 7–8-seriate, brilliant red, with a pleasant though not penetrating perfume.

Named for André Du Pont (in place of the bizarre name used by nurseries) who grew it successfully and was responsible for distributing so many fine roses. He was born in the Palatinate in 1756 and died in Paris in 1817.

Rosa Gallica Pontiana.   *Rosier du Pont.*

P.J. Redouté pinx.   Imprimerie de Rémond   Bessin sculp.

ROSA GALLICA LATIFOLIA [Thory var. n.]
'BIG-LEAVED PROVINS ROSE'

Tufted *bush* 0.6–0.9 m high; *branches* numerous; *prickles* dense, fairly short, unequal, weak, almost straight. *Leaflets* 5(–7), dark green, very large, mostly more than 10 cm long and almost 5 cm wide, upperside glabrous, underside paler and tomentose; petioles villous, rough to the touch, rarely armed with 1 or 2 minute prickles; stipules decurrent, acute, with tomentose margins. *Flowers* clustered at the branch tips; peduncles and pedicels densely aciculate; *receptacles* globose or ovoid, aciculate; *sepals* 3 pinnatifid, 2 simple, acute or spatulate, glandular outside, whitish downy within; *petals* 5–6-seriate, deep pink, cordately notched. *Heps* subellipsoidal, bright red.

This rose was raised some years ago from seed by Lelieur in the Royal Garden at Sèvres, and is not yet widely distributed. It is outstanding for the leaves which are almost as large as those of a walnut, reaching maximum size in the shade rather than in the sun.

Rosa Gallica latifolia. *Rosier de Provins a grandes feuilles.*

P. J. Redouté pinx.

Imprimerie de Remond

Langlois sculp.

ROSA SPINULIFOLIA DEMATRIANA [Thory var. n.]
'SPINY-LEAVED ROSE OF DEMATRA'

Bush 0.9–1.2 m tall; *branches* reddish brown; *prickles* solitary, often opposite, 14–16 mm long, straight, little dilated at the base. *Leaflets* 5 (–7), ovate, acute at both ends, upperside bright green and glabrous, underside paler, the veins covered with very many small hooked prickles, margins uneven, ciliate and glandular; petioles villous, with glands and small prickles; stipules acute, gland-edged. *Flowers* solitary at the tips of the laterals; pedicels and ovoid *receptacles* aciculate; *sepals* simple or narrowly pinnulate; *petals* 5, soft pink; *styles* free.

Dematra discovered this rose near Châtel-sur-Montsalvens in Switzerland.

Rosa spinulifolia foxiana [Thory var. n.] commemorates C.J. Fox, the English orator, whose favourite recreation was botany – roses in particular. It grows spontaneously on the margins of woods near Verviers in the Low Countries and was sent to us by Lemanceau in the summer of 1819. The petals are larger and a little brighter red than in *R. s. dematratiana.* It seems identical with *R. pseudobiginosa* Lej. so far as we can judge from herbarium material.

Rosa Spinulifolia Dematratiana.

Rosier Spinulé de Dematra.

J. Redouté pinx.

Imprimerie de Remond

Chapuy sculp.

ROSA BIFERA MACROCARPA [Thory var. n.]
'LELIEUR'S FOUR-SEASONS ROSE'

Branching *shrub* at most 0.75–0.9 m high; *prickles* abundant, reddish, of unequal lengths up to 16 mm, almost straight, little dilated at the base. *Leaflets* 5–7, ovate, rounded at both ends, upperside dark green, underside and margins villous; petioles glandular; stipules divergent, denticulate, gland-edged. *Flowers* 3–6, corymbose, 20–30(–40) together at the branch tips, deliciously scented; pedicels prickly below, transitional to the funnel-shaped *receptacles*, both these and the pinnatifid sepals densely and fragrantly glandular hispid; bracts elongated ovate, glabrous above, covered below and on the margins with brown, sessile or stalked glands; *petals* 4–5-seriate, pale pink, yellow towards the base, cordately notched, those at the centre curled and crumpled; styles distinct, villous. *Heps* stout and much more elongated than in other variants of *R. bifera*.

This was obtained from seed some years ago in the Royal Garden at Sèvres by Lelieur, author of a valuable treatise on the rose in 1811. It makes a beautiful shrub covered in blooms from May to the end of July, but it should be grown in the shade. It is extremely prolific, and late in the season one finds whole branches in which every bud yields a flower.

Rosa Bifera macrocarpa.　　　*La Quatre Saisons Lelieur.*

P.J. Redouté pinx.　　　　Imprimerie de Remond.　　　　Victor sculp.

ROSA MYRIACANTHA
'THOUSAND-SPINED ROSE'

Differs, according to De Candolle, from *R. pimpinellifolia* by the stiff, straight *stems* bearing short, leafy, one-flowered laterals; the *prickles* half as long again and more numerous; the bidentate *leaflets* being half the size and glandular on the underside and margins; the short glandular hairs on the petioles; the leaf dentition; the glandular hispid pedicels; the small *flowers* not above 2 cm diameter, and above all by the *sepals*.

Indigenous to the Dauphiné and near Montpellier in dry stony places, it remains unchanged by years of cultivation. It has been considered a variety near *R. spinosissima*, and is indeed related, but it is in no way close to *R. villosa* as Lapeyrouse claims. (De Candolle).

Our plant died in the winter of 1819 because we had neglected to cover it. *R. myriacantha magna* Desv. is a variety with larger leaves, glabrous calyx and fewer prickles.

Rosa Myriacantha.

Rosier à Mille-Epines.

P. J. Redouté pinx.

Imprimerie de Remond.

Chapuy sculp.

ROSA DAMASCENA CELSIANA PROLIFERA
'PROLIFEROUS CELS'S ROSE'

Shrub about 0.9 m high; *prickles* short, unequal. Otherwise it is exactly like 'Cels's Rose' (Vol.1 p. 166), differing only in the proliferous blooms. The first is borne on a long peduncle which continues the main axis; the second is on a shorter pedicel from the centre of the bloom. Between bracts and receptacle are variously shaped abortive leaves. Reproductive organs are absent or so deformed as to be unrecognisable.

A seedling from 'Cels's Rose' gave these very full blooms which become leafily proliferous. Such transient freaks do not constitute true varieties because they cannot be perpetuated even by grafting, but we felt it would please readers to see one example of this phenomenon which can be encountered in other species, notably of the Gallicae. According to the botanists, proliferation of rose blooms is occasioned by too lush culture or over-manuring, but it is recognised today that such changes can be independent of the environment, and very full blooms are most prone to them. Linnaeus, who hated double flowers, probably because they defied classification, dismissed them as monstrosities.

Proliferous roses are, in general, borne on bare pedicels, but more rarely, as in the specimen figured, these are leafy. Linnaeus knew proliferation only in *Rosa*, *Anemone* and a few other plants. Today, thanks to the work of gardeners looking for double flowers, it is common, above all in the rose. We have seen in a gallica up to four blooms looking as if threaded one above the other, and the rose named after the Duchess of Berry is only a proliferant that may never be seen again.

Rosa Damascena Celsiana prolifera. *Rosier de Cels a fleurs prolifères.*

P. J. Redouté pinx.   Imprimerie de Remond.   Langlois sculp.

ROSA ALPINA DEBILIS [Thory var. n.]
'DECUMBENT ALPINE ROSE'

Stems glabrous, reddish, slender, weak, quite unarmed. *Leaflets* 7(–9), smaller than in other varieties of *R. alpina*, ovate, green on both surfaces, bidentate; petioles slightly hispid; stipules broad, dilated, denticulate. *Flowers* 1–3 on the laterals; pedicels slightly hispid, straight; bracts basal; *receptacles* ovoid, hispid; *sepals* entire, linear, sometimes spatulate; *petals* 5, large, bright red, whitening towards the base, cordately notched; *styles* pubescent.

This is merely a degeneration of *R. alpina vulgaris*, differing only by the slender, weak, almost recumbent stems, smaller leaflets and larger petals. We found it some years ago in a thicket in Vilmorin's garden, where it had no doubt arisen from a chance seed from the 'Alpine Rose'.

Rosa Alpina debilis. *Rosier des Alpes à tiges foibles.*

P.J. Redouté pinx.   Imprimerie de Remond   Bessin sculp.

ROSA ALBA FOLIACEA [Thory var. n.]
'LEAFY WHITE ROSE OF FLEURY'

Branched *shrub* about 0.9 m high, almost unarmed. *Leaflets* 5, rather rounded, irregularly serrate, upperside pale green and glabrous, underside paler and tomentose; petioles with small, yellowish, recurved *prickles*; stipules denticulate, gland-edged. *Flowers* in threes at the branch tips, sweetly scented; pedicels long, finely bristly and rough to the touch; *corolla* more than 7.5 cm in diameter; *petals* 5–6-seriate, dull white, cordately notched, those at the centre curled and crumpled, overlying the stamens and styles; *receptacles* ovoid, glabrous; *sepals* very long, much exceeding the bud, 2 simple and acute, 3 leafy, reflexed at anthesis, long persistent, not affecting the shape or bulk of the receptacle as in other roses showing the same phenomenon. *Heps* ellipsoidal, red.

This rose was raised from seed in a garden at Fleury-sous-Meudon, where we saw it last summer, and is now being multiplied among amateurs by grafting. The striking white of the blooms, their bulk, and the long leafy sepals which constantly crown them distinguish this cultivar well from all other albas. A sheltered site is needed for it.

Rosa alba foliacea.

La Blanche foliacée de fleury.

P. J. Redouté pinx.

Imprimerie de Remond

Victor sculp.

ROSA EGLANTERIA LUTEOLA [Thory var. n.]
'CANARY YELLOW ROSE'

Much branched *shrub* about 0.9 m tall, similar to the 'Yellow Rose' of which we have given a figure, but smaller in all its parts and with the *stems* covered in a great number of prickles of different sizes. *Leaflets* 7–9(–11), rather dark green, small, subrotund, glabrous on both surfaces, serrulate, gland-edged; petioles glabrous, with small, yellowish prickles; stipules broadening above, gland-edged. *Flowers* 1–2 at the ends of the laterals, unpleasantly scented, but less foetid than those of *R. eglanteria punicea*; *receptacles* depressed globose, glabrous; pedicels long, glabrous; *sepals* entire or pinnatifid, downy within, densely covered with glands outside, *petals* 5, rather small, canary yellow, cordately notched.

Du Pont's 'Tulip Rose' (*R. eglanteria tulipa*) is a derivative of this. They grow in France, England, Germany, Italy and Spain.

Rosa Eglanteria Luteola.

L'Eglantier Serin.

P. J. Redouté pinx.

Imprimerie de Rémond.

Langlois sculp.

ROSA LHERITIERANEA [Thory hybr. n.]
'L'HERITIER'S ROSE'

Profusely blooming *shrub* capable of reaching great height when supported; adult *branches* glabrous; *prickles* sparse, fairly stout, recurved, absent on inflorescences. *Leaflets* 5 or 7, large, acute, rounded at the base, glabrous on both surfaces, uniformly serrate, upperside glossy; petioles glabrous; stipules broad, decurrent, denticulate, with a sessile reddish gland on each tooth. *Flowers* clustered on the ends of the laterals; pedicels glandular hispid; bracts acute ovate, a little glandular at the tip; *sepals* acute, downy within, glandular outside; *petals* 4–5-seriate, incurved over the stamens almost as in the 'Anemone Centifolia' or 'Anemone Sweetbriar', pink tinged violet, whitening towards the base and for the most part traversed inside by a more or less regular whitish line; *stamens* numerous, unequal; *styles* short, distinct. *Heps* ovoid, red.

This fine rose is obviously a hybrid of *R. alpina* and *R. indica*, having been raised from seeds of the latter by Vilmorin about twelve years ago. The beauty of its blooms combined with the elegant habit have made it fairly common in amateur collections. We do not know if it comes true from seed. Up to the present we have only seen it grafted on *R. rubrifolia*, which seems to suit it well. It is well suited for covering arbours and tunnels. We have named it after L'Heritier (1746-1800), to whom Redouté dedicates this modest monument in tribute to his patronage and tuition at the start of his career.

Rosa l'heritieranea.   *Rosier l'héritier.*

P. J. Redouté pinx.   Imprimerie de Rémond.   Victor sculp.

ROSA PIMPINELLIFOLIA INERMIS
'THORNLESS BURNET ROSE'

Stems 0.9 m high, unarmed except in extreme youth when minute, ephemeral prickles are to be seen. *Leaflets* 7, 9 or 11, rounded ovate, simply dentate, glabrous on both surfaces; petioles glabrous; stipules acute. *Flowers* solitary at the tips of the laterals; *receptacles* and pedicels glabrous; *sepals* glabrous, narrow, equal, entire; *petals* 5, fairly large, light to darker red; *stamens* short; *stigmas* amassed in a convex head. *Heps* as for other varieties of *R. pimpinellifolia*.

Nestler found this wild in the Vosges and sent it to De Candolle. It commonly turns up in sowings of seed of the prickly *pimpinellifolia*, and vice versa. It is sought after by amateurs and found in many gardens. It needs no special care, but requires full sun.

Rosa Pimpinelli-folia inermis.   *Rosier Pimprenelle à tiges sans épines.*

P. J. Redouté pinx.   Imprimerie de Remond.   Langlois sculp.

ROSA RUBIGINOSA ANEMONEFLORA
'ANEMONE-FLOWERED SWEETBRIAR'

Bush 0.6–0.9 m high; *prickles* unequal, distant, infrastipular on the stems and adult branches, very numerous and dense on current shoots. *Leaflets* 5 or 7, subrotund, green, bidentate, wine-scented, upperside almost glabrous, underside and margins glandular; petioles villous, glandular, a little prickly; stipules denticulate. *Flowers* 3 or more, subcorymbose at the branch tips; pedicels glandular hispid; *receptacles* ovoid, subglabrous; *sepals* long, appendiculate, tomentose within, covered outside with many sessile glands, falling before the hep ripens; *petals* almost 4-seriate, cordately notched, purple shading towards violet, the innermost shorter, concave, inflexed over the stamens as in the 'Anemone Centifolia'. *Heps* hispid, red blackening in the cool autumn air.

A modification of *R. rubiginosa triflora* Willd. and closely related to Rau's *R. rubiginosa* β. It differs only in its larger size and semi-double blooms in which the petals inflex like an anemone. We saw it for the first time grafted in Catel's garden in 1819, and later on its own roots in other collections. We recommend grafting on common sweetbriar to give maximum volume and darker colouring. Do not prune: merely remove dead wood.

Rosa Rubiginosa anemone-flora.　　　　*Rosier Rouillé à fleurs d'anemone.*

P.J. Redouté pinx.　　　　Imprimerie de Remond.　　　　Langlois sculp.

ROSA BISERRATA
'BIDENTATE MOUNTAIN ROSE'

Stems 0.9–1.2 m high; *prickles* curved, longer than they are high. *Leaflets* ovate, fairly large, glabrous, biserrate, each tooth tipped by a gland; petioles glabrous, little or not at all prickly, slightly glandular; stipules very glandular. *Flowers* solitary, pale pink, in June; pedicels glabrous; *sepals* almost simple, very glandular. *Heps* stout, subglobose, glabrous.

Dr. Mérat found this rose at Mount Valérien near Paris, growing along the walls of the hilltop shrine, and the above description is taken from his Flora. It is strongly related to *R. montana* Villars, *trachyphylla* Rau and *adenophylla* Willd., from which it differs only by the subglobose receptacles and glabrous pedicels. *R. malmundariensis* Le Jeune differs only by its smaller ellipsoidal heps. Otherwise they all appear to derive from *R. montana*. We do not know why Desvaux associated *R. biserrata* with *R. sepium*, which has leaflets glabrous on the upperside and glandular on the underside and margins.

Given the quantity of heps it provides, and its location, we can well believe that the inhabitants of Paris, who before the reign of Henri III went in procession at certain seasons to the shrine or different chapels in the woods around the city, brought back heps of this and other wild roses which at the period were cried in the streets of Paris. (See Villeneuve's poem "Street Cries of Paris".)

Rosa Biserrata.

Rosier des Montagnes a folioles bidentees.

P. J. Redouté pinx.

Imprimerie de Remond.

Chapuy Sculp.

ROSA GALLICA AURELIANENSIS [Thory var. n.]
'DUCHESS OF ORLEANS ROSE'

Bush 0.9–1.2 m tall; *branches* in their upper part covered in numerous, small, reddish, unequal prickles mixed with glands, the lower part with only a few prickles which soon drop off. *Leaflets* 3–5 (–7), large, firm, acute, rounded at the base, irregularly dentate, teeth ciliate, not glandular, upperside glabrous, underside villous; petioles very shortly downy and with some prickles; stipules acute. *Flowers* in threes at the branch tips, faintly scented; pyriform *receptacles* and pedicels glandular hispid; *sepals* downy within, hispid outside; *petals* 5–6-seriate, of a beautiful rather dark pink. *Heps* red.

The elegant stance and size and beauty of the blooms, which develop late and outlast all other roses, distinguish this from the other gallicas. No special care is needed, but it relishes sun and watering. It is rare in collections, but fine grafted specimens can be seen in the Royal Garden at Sèvres. Redouté dedicates it respectfully to the Duchess of Orleans.

Rosa Gallica Aurelianensis   *La Duchesse d'Orléans.*

P. J. Redouté pinx.   Imprimerie de Rémond   Langlois sculp.

ROSA STYLOSA
'UPRIGHT FIELD ROSE'

Bush 1.2–1.5 m tall; *branches* tortuous, greyish; *prickles* hooked, dilated at the base. *Leaflets* 5 or 7, the odd one perfectly ovate, the others ovate and acute at both ends, serrate, upperside glabrous and glossy, underside paler and slightly pubescent; petioles slightly tomentose, with some prickles; stipules rather small, microscopically gland-edged. *Flowers* many together in clusters, lateral and terminal; *receptacles* elongated ovoid, glabrous as are the pedicels; *sepals* 2 simple and 3 pinnatifid, much longer than the unexpanded petals which are 5, cordately notched, soft pink fading rapidly in the sun; *styles* aggregated into a short column as in *R. arvensis*. *Heps* ellipsoidal, red.

This differs from *R. arvensis* by having erect stems which are not stoloniferous, and by the long pinnatifid sepals. Desvaux's *stylosa* has pubescent, unarmed petioles and almost solitary flowers. De Candolle's has the leaves pubescent on both surfaces and flowers solitary or in a small corymb. Both these have white flowers, whereas ours, from hedgerows in Longjumeau and Meudon, has soft pink – again the only difference from *R. stylosa* Loiseleur.

Rosa Stylosa. *Rosier des Champs a tiges érigées.*

P. J. Redouté pinx. Imprimerie de Rémond Chapuy sculp.

ROSA CENTIFOLIA MINOR [Thory var. n.]
'BORDEAUX ROSE'

Shrublet about 45 cm tall; *prickles* unequal, sharp, a little recurved, little dilated at the base, mixed with pedicellate glands, mainly concentrated towards the tops of the branches. *Leaflets* 5 or 7, medium-sized, subrotund, crenate with ciliate and glandular margins, upperside bright green, underside paler and tomentose; petioles villous, unarmed; stipules decurrent, acute, gland-edged. *Flowers* 4–6 at the branch tips; peduncle and pedicels glandular hispid up to one third of the way up the *receptacles; sepals* 2 simple, 3 pinnatifid, glandular outside, villous within; *petals* 7–8-seriate as in common *centifolia*, but flowers smaller. *Heps* as in *centifolia*.

This dwarf rose suckers freely to form thickets, and should be kept in check annually. The flower is in no way different from that of *R. centifolia* and in a good soil the first blooms may be as large. Paris nurserymen grow it in frames, and thus kept it is one of the first to appear in spring in the flower market. Seed raised from it has produced many very lovely novelties.

Rosa Centifolia Burgundiaca.   *La Cent-feuilles de Bordeaux.*

P. J. Redouté pinx.   Imprimerie de Remond.   Langlois sculp.

ROSA GALLICA AGATHA PARVULA VIOLACEA
Lit. 'SMALL RANUNCULUS VIOLET PROVINS AGATHA ROSE'

Shrub up to 45 cm tall; *branches* diffuse, covered in the upper part with very numerous acicles and in the lower part with a few parse unequal *prickles* mixed with glands. *Leaves* inclined in a remarkable way; *leaflets* 5(–7), elliptic, bidenticulate, upperside green and glabrous, underside paler; petioles glandular hispid, with small straight prickles. *Flowers* 1(–2), lateral and terminal, small; *sepals* pinnatifid, short, scarcely overtopping the petals in bud; *petals* 8–10-seriate, purple to dark violet, paler towards the base, densely packed like those of a double *Ranunculus*. *Heps* pyriform, red or dark orange, persisting throughout much of the winter.

This is a variant of the 'Provins Rose' in the Agatha Group, having very double blooms with densely packed petals curled and crumpled at the centre. We found it last summer in Le Dru's rich collection, and amateurs can obtain it from Vibert's nursery. It seems related to Descemet's seedling 'Petite Violette', but the rose under discussion is a little larger. It requires shade and only ordinary culture. Le Dru prunes it very hard.

Rosa Gallica agatha. (Varietas parva violacea.) *La petite Renoncule violette.*

P. J. Redouté pinx. Imprimerie de Rémond Lemaire sculp.

ROSA DAMASCENA ITALICA [Thory var. n.]
'ITALIAN FOUR-SEASONS ROSE'

Sparse *bush* about 0.6 m high; *prickles* very numerous, small, short, unequal, almost straight. *Leaflets* 5 or 7, large, ovate, bright green, simply serrate, upperside glabrous, underside and margins paler and slightly tomentose; petioles villous, with small, yellowish prickles; stipules fairly broad, acute, gland-edged. *Flowers* in threes at the tips of the branches; bracts subtending the lateral pedicels elongated, acute; pedicels and *receptacles* glandular hispid; *sepals* longer than the petals in bud, 3 pinnatifid, 2 simple; *petals* 4–5-seriate, large, soft pink, paler towards the base, cordately notched. *Heps* elongated ovoid, red.

This rose distinguishes itself among the damascenas by the large size of the flowers, often over 7.5 cm in diameter, but only on its own roots since the size is noticeably smaller in grafted specimens. Du Pont received it from Florence twenty years ago and distributed it. It has little perfume, but makes up for this by its grace and elegance. Although long known, it is still rare, but can be seen grafted in Catel's fine collection. On its own roots it is tender and needs full sun.

Rosa Damascena Italica.   *La Quatre-Saisons d'Italie.*

P. J. Redouté pinx.   Imprimerie de Remond   Victor sculp.

ROSA GALLICA AGATHA DELPHINIANA [Thory var. n.]
'CHILD OF FRANCE'

Bush about 0.9 m high; *branches* with many, small, unequal, almost straight prickles, especially in their upper part, mixed with pedicellate glands. *Leaflets* 5, rather dark green, small, oblong ovate, rounded at the base, acute at the tip, upperside glabrous, underside and margins slightly tomentose; petioles glandular, with small, very short prickles; stipules decurrent, acute, gland-edged. *Flowers* 2(–3) at the branch tips; *receptacles* and pedicels reddish glandular hispid; *sepals* 3 pinnatifid, 2 simple, glandular outside, whitish woolly within; *petals* very numerous and densely packed, rather dark pink, overlapping in the fashion of a military pompon, entirely hiding the sepals. *Heps* pyriform, red.

Remarkable both for the beauty and singularity of its blooms, this was introduced about 1802 by Du Pont, who claims that it was known during the reign of Louis XV and that the Dutch dedicated it to the Dauphin, whence the name 'Child of France'. It is rare on its own roots but mostly encountered grafted on sweetbriar. Our picture comes from a beautiful specimen in the Royal Garden at Sèvres.

Rosa Gallica agatha (var. Delphiniana). *L'Enfant de France.*

P.J. Redouté pinx.   Imprimerie de Rémond.   Bessa Sculp.

ROSA INDICA STELLIGERA [Thory var. n.]
'STARRY CHINA ROSE'

Shrublet 20–25 cm high forming a fairly tufted bush, unarmed or with 1–2 prickles near to soil level. *Leaflets* 3 or 5, rounded at the base, pointed at the tip, upperside glabrous and clear green, underside and margins paler, sometimes flushed reddish; petioles purplish, a little hispid, prickly; stipules acute, denticulate. *Flowers* solitary at the branch tips; *receptacles* ovoid, glabrous as are the pedicels; *sepals* entire, spatulate or leafy-tipped, flushed purple outside; *petals* 5, cordately notched, pale pink fading to white towards the base but after 2-3 days uniformly purple as in *R. indica linneana*. *Heps* ellipsoidal, red, a little orange at maturity.

This differs from *R. indica linneana* only by the initially bicolour petals and lower stems which are almost entirely unarmed. We obtained it from seed of *R. indica linneana* in 1819. Like all roses of this group it roots easily from cuttings, but needs shelter in winter.

Rosa Indica Stelligera.　　　　　　　　*Le Bengale Etoilé.*

P. J. Redouté pinx .　　　　　Imprimerie de Rémond　　　　　Chapuy sculp.

ROSA INDICA SERTULATA
'CLUSTERED CHINA ROSE'

Bush 30–38 cm tall; *prickles* not numerous, hooked, fairly stout, little dilated at the base, absent from the inflorescences. *Leaflets* 3 or 5, medium-sized, upperside dark green, underside glaucous and more or less purple flushed even on the margins; petioles reddish, glabrous, prickly; stipules acute, gland-edged. *Flowers* 5–6 at the tips of the laterals, clustered; *receptacles* quite glabrous, subglobose; pedicels long, glandular hispid, especially towards the top; *sepals* entire, acute or spatulate, glabrous outside, tomentose within; *petals* 5–6-seriate, concave, irregularly notched, of a very delicate pink whitening towards the base.

Rosa indica sertulata is distinct from *R. i. subalba* by the globose (not ovoid) receptacle, glandular hispid (not glabrous) pedicels, fast pink (not fading) petals and simple (not pinnate) sepals. It was apparently raised from seed many years ago in the royal nursery at Trianon. For long rare, it is found today in some collections. It is propagated from cuttings rather than grafts, raised in peaty soil in a pot to facilitate bringing in for the winter, since it is the most tender of all the Chinas.

Rosa Indica Sertulata.

Le Bengale à Bouquets.

P.J. Redouté pinx.

Imprimerie de Remond.

Langlois sculp.

ROSA GALLICA AGATHA REGALIS
'ROYAL AGATHA'

Bush about 75 cm high; branches dense, slender, especially in the upper part armed with short, unequal prickles, the larger dilated at the base. *Leaflets* 5(–7), firm, subrotund, bidentate, the teeth sometimes tipped with small glands, upperside glabrous, underside tomentose; petioles somewhat villous, with small prickles; stipules decurrent, acute. *Flowers* medium-sized, often in a cluster at the branch tips; *receptacles* subovoid, subglabrous; pedicels glandular hispid; *corolla* very double; *petals* rather bright pink, those at the centre curled and crumpled; *stamens* absent; *styles* partly free, partly fasciculate.

'Royal Agatha' flowers in early spring and continues for a long time. The outer petals are often flushed whitish or darker red, giving an attractive look to the bloom. 'Provence Agatha' (*R. provincialis incarnata*) is only a paler derivative, as is probably Andrews's 'Belle-Fille' (*R. belladonna*).

Rosa Gallica-Agatha. (Var. Regalis.)   *Rosier Agathe-Royale.*

P.J. Redouté pinx.   Imprimerie de Remond.   Langlois sculp.

ROSA GALLICA AGATHA PROLIFERA
'PROLIFEROUS AGATHA'

Absolutely similar to the preceding, except for the slightly paler flower from the centre of which comes a second, and from that sometimes even a third. These open successively, albeit badly. In this monstrosity the pedicel is flattened and commonly provided with long leafy bracts arranged in tiers: a case of leafy proliferation. Sometimes 4–5 buds can be seen coming from one axis, depending on the vigour of the plant. In contrast, in a dry summer, only one or two among all the blooms proliferate. Invariably the bud is flattened and as if incised at the top.

The Agatha roses have produced very many derivatives which are much sought after for their great floriferousness. A list is appended of the garden names of 38 of these. The differences between them are very fine – notably the habit and petal colour and differentia equally trivial in the eyes of botanists. However, we think that a massed display of Agatha roses, grafted on sweetbriar 0.6–0.9 m tall, closely planted and arranged in tiers, would give a fine effect, the more so since these shrubs, which almost all flower at the same time, would offer an immense quantity of very double blooms of varying shades lasting for over a month.

Rosa Gallica Agatha (var. Prolifera.)

Rosier Agathe Prolifère.

P. J. Redouté pinx.

Imprimerie de Remond.

Victor sculp.

ROSA GALLICA FLORE MARMOREO
'SPECKLED PROVINS ROSE'

Bush 0.9–1.2 m high; *prickles* small, short, unequal, almost straight, very dense, mainly on the flowering branches. *Leaflets* 5 or 7, mostly rounded ovate, upperside green, underside paler; petioles slightly tomentose, with many small recurved prickles; stipules fairly broad, acute. *Flowers* almost scentless, 7.5 cm or more in diameter, clustered at the branch tips; *receptacles* ovoid, glabrous or glandular hispid; pedicels wholly covered in short acicles and sessile glands; *sepals* pinnatifid; *petals* 2–3-seriate, pale pink spotted darker pink to give a marbled effect; *stamens* numerous; *stigmas* short, in a sessile hemispherical head.

Seedlings of *R. gallica* not infrequently show marbling of the petals with spots of different shapes and colours. Loiseleur Deslongchamps has described a superb cultivar as 'Pentad Rose' (*R. gallica meleagris*), but we have not cited this in synonymy as it differs from ours in the very fine white spotting of the petals.

Our rose makes a fine display grafted on sweetbriar. It is in demand, not only because of its variegation, but also because it is only semi-double, which amateurs prefer, in general, to single or full blooms.

Rosa Gallica flore marmoreo.   *Rosier de Provins à fleurs marbrées.*

P. Redouté pinx.   Imprimerie de Rémond   Bessin sculp.

ROSA SEPIUM MYRTIFOLIA
'MYRTLE-LEAVED HEDGE ROSE'

Stems 0.9 m high at most, much branched, diffuse, yellowish green, smooth; *branches* weak, almost pendent; *prickles* strong, hooked, fairly dense, sometimes paired at the base of the stipules. *Leaflets* (5–)7, scentless, ovate acute, serrulate, upperside glabrous and almost glossy, underside covered with very short bristles mixed with glands; petioles slightly tomentose, glandular, prickly; stipules decurrent, acute. *Flowers* lateral and terminal, most often solitary at the tips of the laterals; *receptacles* ovoid, glabrous like the pedicels; *sepals* elongated, pinnatifid, smooth outside, slightly woolly within; *petals* 5, whitish, flushed reddish on exposure to the sun; *stamens* numerous; *styles* almost glabrous. *Heps* ellipsoidal, red, blackening at maturity.

This rose is remarkable for its tiny leaves, shiny above and rather like those of myrtle. It differs from *R. sepium* Thuillier by the lower stems and smaller leaflets. It is a little scarcer than others of its group. Haller jun. found it in the Swiss mountains, and we have received it under different names from various departments of France. It is found on the outskirts of woods near Paris and is often confused with typical *sepium*. It favours dry places and flowers, always sparingly, in June and July. Some people cultivate it because of its odd foliage.

Rosa Sepium Myrtifolia.   *Rosier des Hayes à feuilles de Myrte.*

P. J. Redouté pinx.   Imprimerie de Rémond   Langlois sculp.

ROSA GALLICA FLORE GIGANTEO [Thory var. n.]
'GIANT-FLOWERED PROVINS ROSE'

Shrub to o.6 m high; *prickles* many, small, unequal, slightly flexible in the upper parts of the branches; longer, stiff and straight or recurved in the lower parts. *Leaflets* 5 or 7, elongated ovate, acute at the tip, cordate at the base, firm, unequally dentate, some of the teeth gland-tipped, upperside glabrous, underside slightly tomentose; petioles slightly tomentose, with small yellowish prickles; stipules decurrent, denticulate. *Flowers* 1–3 at the branch tips; *receptacles* pyriform, like the pedicels glandular hispid; *sepals* 3 pinnatifid, 2 simple, densely whitish woolly within, minutely bristly and glandular outside; corolla exceeding 12.5 cm in diameter, faintly scented; *petals* many-seriate, pink, irregularly notched, the innermost ones curled and crumpled making it almost impossible to see what remains of the stamens. *Heps* subglobose, fairly stout, red.

This rose, outstanding for its flower size, was raised from seed in 1813 in the Royal Garden at Sèvres, where there are many grafted plants, but it is not yet widespread in gardens. In view of the beauty and extraordinary bulk of the bloom, we ought to consider how we can use seed raising to increase the number of rose-cultivars. Regrettably this method is no longer being used in France, where we are content to propagate by layering and grafting thus achieving only the slavish multiplication of identical roses.

Rosa Gallica flore giganteo.　　　　　　*Rosier de Provins a fleur gigantesque.*

P.J. Redouté pinx.　　　　　　*Imprimerie de Rémond*　　　　　　Victor sculp.

ROSA GALLICA STAPELIAEFLORA [Thory var. n.]
'STAPELIA-FLOWERED PROVINS ROSE'

Bush about 0.75 m high; *bristles* short and mixed with glands in the upper parts of the branches; *prickles* short, unequal, straight or slightly recurved in the lower parts. *Leaflets* 5, rather small, upperside glabrous, underside tomentose; margins glandular and ciliate; petioles slightly villous and prickly; stipules acute, denticulate. *Flowers* (1–)3 at the branch tips; *receptacles* glabrous; pedicels glandular hispid; *sepals* 3 pinnatifid and 2 simple, downy within, glandular outside; *petals* 5, large, somewhat concave, rather dark purple but partly covered in tiny longitudinal flecks of fawn yellow, reddish or other colours; *stamens* very numerous; *styles* aggregated into a convex head. *Heps* subglobose, reddish turning black at maturity.

The name we have given to this rose derives from the spots covering the petals which recall those of *Stapelia*, although there they lie in transverse bands. Otherwise it is in no way distinct from the ancestral species.

Rosa Gallica Stapelia flora.　　　*Rosier de Provins à fleurs de Stapelie.*

P. J. Redouté pinx.　　　Imprimerie de Remond.　　　Bessin sculp.

ROSA GALLICA ROSEA FLORE SIMPLICI
'SINGLE PROVINS ROSE'

0.6–0.9 m high; *branches* diffuse, with many, small, unequal, slender *prickles* little dilated at the base. *Leaflets* 5, fairly large, in general rounded at the base and apex, upperside green, underside paler and tomentose; margins shortly hairy and glandular; petioles glandular hispid, rarely with small prickles; stipules large, acute, denticulate, gland-edged. *Flowers* 1–3 at the tips of the laterals; pedicels long, glandular hispid; *receptacles* subglobose, glabrous; *sepals* pinnatifid with spatulate pinnules; *corolla* 9 cm in diameter; *petals* 5, pink, cordately notched. *Heps* globose, red.

This rose has been long known and cultivated in England, notably in the garden of Shailer at Little Chelsea. It is also common in Italy and Spain, and we have seen it in Ternaux's rosarium at Auteuil where it was obtained from seed two years ago.

Rosa Gallica rosea flore simplici.   *Rosier de Provins à fleurs roses et simples.*

P.J. Redouté pinx.   Imprimerie de Rémond.   Langlois sculp.

ROSA BIFERA PUMILA [Thory var. n.]
'DWARF FOUR-SEASONS ROSE'

Dwarf *shrub* up to a maximum of 30 cm tall; *prickles* unequal, mostly small and almost straight. *Leaflets* rounded ovate, upperside dark green, underside and margins slightly tomentose; petioles glandular, sometimes with small prickles; stipules denticulate, gland-edged, with diverging tips. *Flowers* compact, strongly perfumed, 3–15 in corymbose clusters; peduncles, pedicels, funnel-shaped *receptacles* and pinnate *sepals* all densely covered in fine bristles and viscous scented glands; bracts elongated, acute, upperside glabrous, underside glandular, margins ciliate; *corolla* medium-sized; *petals* many-seriate, pale pink, cordately notched, those at the centre curled and inflexed over the *styles* which are villous and distinct. *Heps* pyriform, red.

This miniature reached us from the nurseryman Noel of Paris, who raised it from seed. The abundant blooms are well-formed. It is very close to *R. bifera officinalis* and *R. b. myropolarum*, from which it differs only by the dwarf habit and erectly corymbose inflorescences, whereas the others are taller and laxly paniculate.

Rosa Bifera pumila

Le petit Quatre-Saisons

P. J. Redouté pinx.

Imprimerie de Rémond

Lemaire sculp.

ROSA FARINOSA
'FARINOSE ROSE'

Much-branched *shrub* 0.9(–1.5) m tall; *prickles* firm, almost straight, those on current growth smaller and a little recurved, the tips of the shoots being almost unarmed. *Leaflets* 3–5(–7), acute or obtuse, covered on both surfaces with soft, whitish wool, bidentate, the teeth glandular, ciliate; stipules lanceolate, acute, denticulate, upperside glabrous, underside densely glandular and hairy. *Flowers* subcorymbose at the branch tips; pedicels glabrous above, pubescent below; *receptacles* ovoid, glabrous; bracts villous, gland-edged; *sepals* appendiculate, whitish woolly within; *petals* 5, very pale pink, notched, a little longer than the sepals. *Heps* ovoid to subglobose, dull red.

Seen from a distance, this rose seems covered in a whitish powder which could be called a farina – the origin of Rau's name for it. However, we consider it as part of the group *Villosae*, from which it differs only by the receptacle and upper part of the pedicel being glabrous. It grows in Germany near Würzburg.

Rosa farinosa.

Rosier farineux

P.J. Redouté pinx.

Imprimerie de Rémond.

Victor sculp.

ROSA INDICA DICHOTOMA
'ANIMATING CHINA ROSE'

o.6 m high or more if kept in a temperate house; *branches* diffuse, bifurcating; *prickles* sparse, unequal, hooked. *Leaflets* 5(–7), acute or ovate, serrulate, upperside green and glossy, underside paler; petioles slightly tomentose, with small prickles extending up the midribs of the leaflets; stipules narrow, denticulate, acute. *Flowers* scented, clustered at the branch tips on bifurcating, glabrous peduncles; pedicels glandular hispid; *receptacles* globose, glabrous; *sepals* simple or pinnatifid, glandular outside; *petals* many-seriate, dark pink, notched, never expanding well. *Heps* pale red.

This rose comes from England where it is known as 'Animating' ('Animated Rose') and was introduced by Boursault some years ago. The perfume recalls that of *R. indica fragrans*. It only flourishes and develops its dichotomous peduncles well in the protection of a temperate house with free root run, and is consequently rarely seen outdoors. It is easily multiplied from cuttings.

Rosa Indica dichotoma.   *Le Bengale animating.*

P. J. Redouté pinx.   Imprimerie de Rémond.   Chapuy sculp.

ROSA CENTIFOLIA PROLIFERA-FOLIACEA
'LEAFY-PROLIFEROUS CABBAGE ROSE'

o.6 m high on its own roots; *stems* and *foliage* similar to those of *R. centifolia* with the exception of the long *sepals* and proliferating flowers. This combines two cultivars on one plant: the 'Leafy Cabbage Rose' and the 'Proliferous Cabbage Rose'. It is considered to be a modification of *R. centifolia gigantea* or *pictorum*, which are much esteemed for the largest flowers of the group and for their fragrance. The monstrous growth of this rose is a product of soil quality, fertiliser, atmospheric conditions, frequent watering and other circumstances. Nevertheless, growers cannot rely on success for their pains – often only ordinary flowers are the outcome. Du Pont grows it but does not list it because of these continual vagaries.

Although up to now the *centifolia* roses seem to excel all others, Guerrapain prefers the *biferas* ('Four Seasons'), criticising the Cabbage Roses for forming less shapely bushes, sparse foliage to accompany the blooms, less shapely and elegant buds, less delicate perfume, and for a tendency to canker and die back on old wood.

Rosa Centifolia prolifera foliacea.   *La Cent-feuilles prolifère foliacée.*

P. J. Redouté pinx.   Imprimerie de Remond   Victor sculp.

ROSA COLLINA MONSONIANA
'LADY MONSON'S ROSE'

Shrub 0.9 m or more high; *branches* slender, glabrous; *prickles* stout, hooked. *Leaflets* 5–7, ovate, rounded at the base, acute at the apex, upperside glabrous, underside and margins slightly pubescent; petioles glandular hispid, with small, hooked, yellowish prickles; stipules denticulate, gland-edged. *Flowers* many together at the tips of the laterals; *receptacles* ovoid, glabrous; pedicels glandular hispid; bracts elongated, ovate, gland-edged; *sepals* 3 pinnatifid, 2 simple, downy within, glandular outside; *petals* 5, rather large, notched, clear pink; *styles* short, united by their stigmas but not coherent. *Heps* orange-red.

We owe this rose to Sabine, Secretary of the Horticultural Society of London who found it in Lady Monson's garden. *R. systyla* and *canina* are distinct from it by their leaves being glabrous on both surfaces, and the former also has coherent styles; *montana* differs in having leaflets ciliate and glandular only on the margins. *R. collina monsoniana* seems to be related to *R. andegavensis* Bastard, having also a glandular hispid pedicel, but the latter has wholly glabrous leaflets.

Rosa Collina Monsonia.   *Le Rosier de Ladi-Monson*

P.J. Redouté pinx.   Imprimerie de Reimond.   Langlois Sculp.

ROSA INDICA CARYOPHILLEA [Thory var. n.]
'CARNATION CHINA ROSE'

Elegant *shrub* 38–50 cm high; *prickles* rather small and recurved on adult branches; inflorescences generally unarmed. *Leaflets* 5, glabrous, glandular crenate, the odd one very acute, upperside green, underside paler; petiole glandular with small reddish hooked prickles below; stipules acute, denticulate. *Flowers* faintly scented, almost as double as those of the 'Hundred-petalled China Rose', in threes at the branch tips; *receptacles* ovoid, glabrous, longitudinally grooved; peduncles glabrous; pedicels glandular hispid; bracts ["stipules" by error] long, narrow; *sepals* simple, acute, gland-edged; *petals* 8–10-seriate, rather dark pink, some traversed by a white line right from the base to the tip, irregularly notched, crumpled and folded so that the flower at the peak of development resembles a carnation. *Heps* ovoid to subglobose, glabrous.

Redouté raised this from seeds of the Common China. It is quite distinct from all others by its carnation-pink colour and the singular form of the petals, which give it its name. Its cultivation is the same as for other Chinas, and it should be kept in a pot and taken under cover for the winter.

Rosa Indica Caryophyllea.　　　　*La Bengale Oeillet.*

P.J. Redouté pinx.　　　Imprimerie de Rémond.　　　Langlois sculp.

ROSA RUBIFOLIA
'BRAMBLE-LEAVED ROSE'

Shrub 0.9–1.2 m tall; *prickles* small, reddish, hooked, sparse, sometimes infrastipular. Leaflets 3–5, soft and seemingly puckered, unequally dentate, upperside glabrous and clear green; underside paler and tomentose; petioles glandular and prickly; stipules reddish, denticulate. *Flowers* clustered at the branch tips, the long pedicels and globose receptacles being glandular hispid; bracts long, sometimes leafy, gland-edged; *sepals* short, with filiform pinnules, glandular outside, slightly tomentose within; *petals* 5, soft pink fading to white, cordately notched, mucronate; *stamens* very numerous; *styles* coherent into a glabrous column like *R. arvensis*.

Quite a new rose for France, to which a living root was sent by Sabine, it is a member of De Candolle's *Synstilae*. Lindley makes Donn's *R. fenestrata* a variety of his *R. fenestralis*, which differs from *R. rubifolia* only by the completely glabrous leaflets and solitary flowers.

Rosa Rubifolia.   *Rosier à feuilles de Ronce.*

P. J. Redouté pinx.   Imprimerie de Remond   Victor sculp.

ROSA EGLANTERIA SUBRUBRA [Thory var. n.]
Lit. 'CHERRY BRIAR' ['AUSTRIAN COPPER']

Shrub 0.6–0.9 m high; *prickles* very short and recurved on the old wood; inflorescences unarmed. *Leaflets* 7, small, glabrous on both surfaces, elliptic, unequally dentate, upperside glaucous green, underside paler; petioles glabrous; stipules dilated, acute, margins slightly ciliate. *Flowers* solitary at the tips of the laterals; *receptacles* globose, a little depressed at the base, glabrous; pedicels shortly bristly and glandular; *sepals* entire, acute, shorter than the petals, glabrous outside, villous within; *petals* 5, cordately notched, pale cherry red within, canary yellow outside, light at the apex and very marked towards the base; *stamens* numerous; *styles* villous, fasciculate; *stigmas* and *anthers* yellow.

It is most likely that this has been obtained from seed of the yellow *R. eglanteria punicea*, but it differs in the following ways as well as in flower colour:

1. The flowering branches are unarmed, not prickly;
2. The leaves are glaucous, not grass green; the petioles are glabrous and not hispid; the pedicels are glandular hispid, not glabrous;
3. The stigmas are pure yellow, not bright purple-red.

The rose is not common in gardens. We saw it in Vilmorin's nursery some years ago.

Rosa Eglanteria sub rubra.

L. Eglantier Cerise.

P.J. Redouté pinx.   Imprimerie de Rémond.   Langlois sculp.

ROSA CANINA GRANDIFLORA [Thory var. n.]
'BIG-FLOWERED DOG ROSE'

Branched *shrub* 0.9–1.2 m tall; *prickles* strong, recurved, often whorled below the stipules. *Leaflets* 3–5(–7), glabrous on both surfaces, upperside green, underside paler; petioles with small prickles, glandular hispid as are the midribs and sometimes the lateral ribs also; stipules narrow, acute, denticulate, ciliate, gland-edged. *Flowers* (1–)3, mostly at the tips of the laterals; peduncles and pedicels glandular hispid; bracts opposite, ciliate, gland-edged; *receptacles* subglobose, glabrous; *sepals* 3 pinnatifid, with short spatulate pinnules, 2 simple; *petals* 5, larger than in other Caninae, soft pink, yellowing towards the base, irregularly notched; *styles* forming a sessile head. *Heps* subglobose, red.

This attractive variant was found last year by Lemeunier in La Flèche, and a root given us flowered in spring in our garden. It is distinct from all other *caninas* by the type of glaucous farina covering the flower before anthesis, the size of petals and their brilliance – which circumstance led Lemeunier to suggest the name *R. canina fulgens*. However, in choosing a name we thought the size of the bloom a more immediately obvious and characteristic feature.

Rosa Canina grandiflora.   *Rosier Canin à grandés fleurs.*

P. J. Redouté pinx.   Imprimerie de Remond.   Lemaire sculp.

ROSA GALLICA AGATHA INCARNATA
'PINK AGATHA'

Densely branched; *prickles* numerous, especially towards the tops of the branches, unequal, reddish, almost straight. *Leaflets* firm, denticulate, each tooth gland-tipped, upperside dark green, glabrous, underside paler, tomentose. *Flowers* clustered at the branch tips; *petals* very numerous and densely packed, a paler pink than in *R. gallica agatha prolifera. Heps* very rarely set.

This is sometimes confused with *R. alba incarnata* ('La Cuisse de Nymphe Emué'), but that belongs to a different group. It has produced numerous derivatives differing only in the degree of pinkness of the corolla. It blooms at the end of June and is very common in gardens where it was formerly known under the name of 'M. Louise'.

Rosa Gallica Agatha incarnata.

L'Agathe Carnée.

P.J Redouté pinx. Imprimerie de Remond Langlois sculp

ROSA GALLICA MAHEKA FLORE SUBSIMPLICI
'NEAR-SINGLE MAHEKA'

Too well known to require a description, this is one of the most magnificent of all the gallicas. It demands no special care, needing only exposure to full sun to bring out the full brilliance of the colours. Rather rarely completely single flowers can be found on it. It came to us from Dutch nurseries almost thirty years ago and was distributed by Du Pont. Several gardeners refer to it as [Lit.] 'The Fair Sultana'.

Rosa Gallica Maheka. (flore subsimplici).   *Le Maheka à fleurs simples.*

P. J. Redouté pinx.   Imprimerie de Remond.   Langlois sculp.

ROSA RECLINATA [Thory hybr. n.] *FLORE SIMPLICI*
[Lit.] 'SINGLE DROOP-BUD ROSE' and
ROSA RECLINATA FLORE SUBMULTIPLICI
[Lit.] 'NEAR-DOUBLE DROOP-BUD ROSE'

(Facing page and following page.)

These two roses require only a single description since they are identical except that one has five, the other about 20, petals. Both can reach a great height if supported; *branches* unarmed or occasionally with prickles on the lower part. *Leaflets* (3–)7, glabrous, simply dentate, upperside clear green, underside paler; petioles glabrous, with small reddish prickles; stipules decurrent, acute, denticulate, flushed red in youth, later greenish. *Flowers* mostly clustered at the tips of the laterals, the buds facing downwards at first but becoming erect at anthesis; *receptacles* short, subglobose, glabrous like the pedicels and calyx; *sepals* subsimple, as long as the petals, spatulate; *petals* cordately notched, pale pink. *Heps* subglobose, red.

The rose with single flowers is probably a hybrid between the China Rose and the Alpine Rose: it was sent to us by Cugnot and is rather rare. The second, known as the 'Boursault Rose' and commonly found in gardens, came from seed of the foregoing. Both are covered in spring with a great number of blooms which persist up to the autumn on favourably sited plants. No special care is needed.

Rosa Reclinata flore simplici.   *Rosier à boutons renversés Var: à fleurs simples.*

P. J. Redouté pinx.   Imprimerie de Remond   Bessin sculp.

ROSA RECLINATA FLORE SUBMULTIPLICI
[Lit.] 'NEAR-DOUBLE DROOP-BUD ROSE'

(For descriptive text see previous page.)

Rosa Reclinata flore sub multiplici.　　*Rosier* à boutons penchés. *(var. à fleurs semi doubles.)*

P. J. Redouté pinx.　　Imprimerie de Remond.　　Langlois Sculp.

ROSA HISPIDA ARGENTEA
[Lit.] 'SILVER-FLOWERED HISPID ROSE'

Very tufted *bush* 1.8–2.1 m tall; *branches* hispid with persistent acicles, some pliant, others rigid, and infrequent, almost straight *prickles*, principally on the current wood. *Leaflets* 9–11, small, oblong ovate, bidentate, upperside glabrous, underside slightly tomentose, petioles ["peduncles"] glabrous except for minute prickles; stipules acute. *Flowers* almost always solitary at the tips of the laterals; pedicels and globose *receptacles* glandular hispid; *sepals* very short, entire, similarly hispid outside; *petals* 6–7-seriate, concave, silvery white, cordately notched. *Heps* globose, wholly covered in bristles, reddish.

This differs from *R. pimpinellifolia* by the persistent (not caducous) prickles, the bidentate (not simply dentate) leaflets with tomentose undersides, and the bristly heps. It is the most elegant of all the white-flowered roses, and is covered at the start of June in a profusion of perfectly round blossoms – especially if one avoids pruning. It sometimes performs again in the autumn. Formerly a single-flowered pink cultivar was grown in the Royal Gardens, but it has been lost for a long time now.

Rosa hispida Argentea.　　　　*Rosier hispide à fleurs Argentées.*

P.J. Redouté pinx.　　　　Imprimerie de Rémond　　　　Lemaire Sculp.

ROSA VENTENATIANA [Thory sp. n.]
'VENTENAT'S ROSE'

Sparse *shrub* about 0.6 m high; *prickles* very numerous and dense, small, straight, unequal. *Leaves* early deciduous from the lower parts of the branches, crowded and persistent around the flowers; *leaflets* 3–7, elliptic, finely dentate, glabrous, upperside rather dark green, underside paler; petioles with sessile glands and small, hooked prickles; stipules narrow, reddish. *Flowers* very fragrant, solitary at the branch tips; pedicels prickly and with sessile glands; *receptacles* thimble-shaped, glabrous, flushed reddish at the top, with flexible bristles at the base; *sepals* shorter than petals, entire, acute, purplish outside; *petals* 4–5-seriate, soft pink, yellowish towards the base, cordately notched; *styles* free, almost sessile, fasciculate. *Heps* subglobose, red.

This rose shares with *R. pomponiana* the same habit, scent and leaf rosettes beneath the buds; with *turbinata* the receptacle shape; with *gallica* the armature, and with *bifera* the ability to flower from June to the end of October. It is a true hybrid, but one that reproduces true from seed in its main characters. It is only found grafted in collections. In spite of its fine perfume it ranks below many others because of its poor habit, dropping its leaves often before the buds develop, leaving only clusters persisting around the flowers up to the time of fruit set.

We have dedicated this rose to Étienne Pierre Ventenat (1757-1808), indefatigable botanist, member of the French Institute, author of catalogues of the Vegetable Kingdom, of Cels's plants, of the Malmaison Garden, and so forth.

Rosa Ventenatiana.

Rosier Ventenat.

P. J. Redouté pinx.

Imprimerie de Rémond

Victor sculp.

ROSA BIFERA VARIEGATA [Thory var. n.]
'VARIEGATED FOUR-SEASONS ROSE'

Shrub with numerous, unequal, straight or recurved *prickles*. *Leaflets* subrotund, variegated with random, unequal, yellowish spots, dentition uniform, underside and margins slightly tomentose; petioles hispid, with small very sharp prickles; stipules denticulate. *Flowers* medium-sized, similar to those of other Biferae, very fragrant, almost full, in an erect corymb at the branch tips; *sepals* 3 pinnatifid, 2 simple, margins glandular and ciliate; *petals* 5–6-seriate. *Heps* ellipsoidal, red.

This rose is noteworthy only for the leaf variegation, which often disappears in grafted specimens after two or three years. Hence in order to preserve this beautiful effect the rose must be grafted annually on sweetbriar or, better, on vigorous shoots of *R. bifera*. We received grafts from Goupil jun., a well-informed rose amateur, and from these came the source of our figure.

Rosa Bifera Variegata.   *La Quatre-Saisons à feuilles panachées.*

P. J. Redouté pinx.   Imprimerie de Remond   Victor Sculp.

ROSA SEMPERVIRENS LESCHENAULTIANA [Thory var. n.]
'LESCHENAULT'S ROSE'

Rampant *shrub* attaining 18–21 m when supported; *branches* and foliage glaucous violet; *prickles* sparse. *Leaflets* 5–7, elliptic, obtuse below, acute above, simply denticulate; petioles glandular hispid, with small hooked prickles; stipules decurrent, entire. *Flowers* sweetly scented, clustered at the tips of the laterals; pedicels and ovoid *receptacles* glandular hispid; *sepals* entire, spatulate or acute, sometimes bifid; *petals* 5, large, pure white, cordately notched; *stamens* numerous; *styles* coherent into a column, bristly with yellow hairs; *stigmas* violet.

Leschenault supplied us with this rose which accordingly bears his name. It was found in the Nilgiri Hills, the highest part of the Western Ghats in peninsular India and is related to *R. sempervirens latifolia* (See Vol. 1 p. 162), but this latter is green overall, has a subglabrous receptacle, pinnatifid sepals and often longitudinal reddish stripes on the undersides of the petals. Its native name is 'Samatigné'. In Paris it exists only as dried specimens, and gardeners regret that it has not been possible to bring live plants to Europe.

Rosa sempervirens Leschenaultiana.　　　*Le Rosier Leschenault.*

P.J. Redouté pinx.　　　Imprimerie de Remond.　　　Langlois sculp.

ROSA GALLICA GUERINIANA
'GUERIN'S ROSE'

At most 0.6–0.9 m tall ; adult *branches* with sparse, fairly stout, hooked *prickles*; inflorescences with very numerous, small, almost straight acicles and rather rare prickles slightly shorter than those on the old wood. *Leaflets* 5, bright green, unequally denticulate, upperside glabrous, underside paler; petioles glandular, with prickles often extending up to the midrib of the odd leaflet; stipules acute, denticulate. *Flowers* mostly solitary, at the tips of the laterals; pedicels long, rough from small bristles mixed with sessile glands; *receptacles* globose, glabrous; *sepals* glabrous outside, downy within; *petals* 8–10-seriate, apex a fine violet, base almost pink, irregularly notched, those at the centre curled and crumpled, almost concealing what remains of the stamens. *Heps* red.

'Guerin's Rose' is distinguished from all others by the beauty of the foliage and elegance of the blooms which cover the whole shrub in spring. It was obtained from seed some years ago at Angers by Guerin, a patient and skilful grower, and it is obtainable from his nursery.

Rosa Gallica Gueriniana.　　　　　*Rosier Guerin.*

P. J. Redouté pinx.　　　　Imprimerie de Rémond　　　　Langlois sculp.

ROSA INDICA AUTUMNALIS
'AUTUMN CHINA ROSE'

Bush about 45 cm tall; *prickles* sparse, small, sometimes absent on the inflorescences. *Leaflets* 5, corrugated or rugose as in *R. indica multipetala* but smaller, firm, serrate and glabrous, at first flushed red; petiole undersides with small yellowish prickles; stipules narrow, denticulate. *Flowers* 1–2 at the branch tips; pedicels glandular hispid; *receptacles* roundish turbinate, glabrous; *sepals* entire, acute, glabrous outside, downy within; *petals* 5–6-seriate, pink suffused violet. *Heps* subglobose, red.

This derivative of *R. indica multipetala* covers itself in a multitude of buds in spring and summer, but all abort and fall without opening. Only in the autumn, towards the middle of September, do the buds open completely. Dr. Cartier sent it to us, having raised it from seed in his fine rose garden. It stands frosts well.

Rosa indica Automnalis.   *Le Bengale d'Automne.*

P. J. Redouté pinx.   Imprimerie de Rémond.   Bessin Sculp.

ROSA VILLOSA EVRATHIANA
'EVRATH'S ROSE'

Very vigorous *bush* up to 3 m high; *prickles* generally very few or even absent. *Leaflets* (3–)5–7, very large, upperside glabrous and dark green, underside paler and slightly villous; petioles slightly glandular. *Flowers* in a hanging panicle; pedicels and elongated ovoid *receptacles* densely glandular hispid; *sepals* appendiculate, very long, glandular; *petals* 7–8-seriate, soft pink, scented, but the buds rarely open properly.

Dedicated to Evrath, a distinguished amateur, who received this rose from Dutch nurseries under the name of 'Black Nutmeg'. It has the same receptacle shape as *R. alba*, the villous leaf undersides and glandular inflorescences and receptacles of *R. villosa*, and the inability to open buds as in *R. turbinata* – a mongrel indeed. Nevertheless, Du Pont sees more of *villosa* in it than any other rose, so places it in the Villosae, which opinion we have accepted.

Poiret and Lindley claim this rose as native to Carolina, but it is not listed among the indigenous species by Nuttall in 1818. Bosc considers that it is sufficiently vigorous to be used as a grafting stock to replace sweetbriar which is becoming scarce.

Rosa Evratina. *Rosier d'Evrat.*

P.J. Redouté pinx. Imprimerie de Rémond Langlois Sculp.

ROSA RUBIGINOSA VAILLANTIANA [Thory var. n.]
'VAILLANT'S SWEETBRIAR'

Bush about 75 cm tall; *prickles* sparse, almost straight. *Leaflets* 5 or 7, rather small, green, almost glabrous, upperside almost glossy, underside paler and, like the margins, covered in hairs and russet, scented glands; petioles villous, with small yellowish prickles; stipules denticulate. *Flowers* borne at the tips of the laterals; pedicels and ovoid *receptacles* glandular hispid; *sepals* 3 pinnatifid, 2 simple, with sessile glands outside, whitish downy within; *petals* 5, cordately notched, white very faintly flushed pink on opening but turning pure white after some hours. *Heps* small, ovoid, red.

The persistent white of the corolla up to petal-fall distinguishes this from the other Rubiginosae which are more or less dark red. We have named this rose after Sébastien Vaillant of the Academy of Sciences and Professor of Botany at the Royal Garden, who found it near Paris and included it in his flora published at the start of the eighteenth century. It seemed to be lost, since no author since Vaillant mentioned it, but we have rediscovered it while botanising with the Linnean Society in the Meudon woods on hills adjoining Fleury. It is a wild beauty that will make little display in our gardens and is best left to the woods and rocks.

Rosa Rubiginosa Vaillantiana.

L'Églantine de Vaillant.

P. J. Redouté pinx.
Imprimerie de Rémond.
Victor sculp.

ROSA MUSCOSA ANEMONEFLORA [Thory var. n.]
'MOSS ROSE OF LA FLÈCHE'

Bush 45–50 cm high, perhaps more; young *branches* reddish brown, later greyish; *prickles* very numerous and dense, unequal, straight, extending up to the pedicels. *Leaves* at first strikingly reddish, later green; *leaflets* 5 or 7, dark green, rather small, elongated, acute, base rounded, upperside glabrous, underside and margins densely covered in glands which are often branched. *Flowers* always upright, never inclined as in the common moss rose, (1–) several at the branch tips; *receptacles*, peduncles and pedicels long aciculate; *petals* 4–5-seriate, converging on the centre as in the 'Anemone Centifolia', dark pink, some striped with paler pink or whitish; *stamens* very long. *Heps* not seen.

Le Meunier obtained this from seed and sent it to us requesting that it be named after his home town, La Flèche. It is recognisable at first glance from the common moss rose, and seems to prefer shade, the flowers promptly withering on our two-year-old plant when exposed to full sun.

Rosa Muscosa Anemone-flora.   *La Mousseuse de la Flèche.*

P. J. Redouté pinx.   Imprimerie de Remond   Victor sculp.

ROSA POMPONIANA MUSCOSA [Thory var. n.]
'MOSSY POMPON'

At most 0.3 m tall; *prickles* small, very numerous and dense, unequal, almost straight, mixed with glandular hairs. *Leaflets* 3 or 5, upperside glabrous, underside, margins and petioles glandular. *Flowers* 2–3 at the tips of the branches; whole inflorescence up to the sepals covered in viscous, branched, moss-like glands; bracts much elongated, spatulate and leafy at the tip; *petals* around 8–10-seriate, the same colour as the ordinary 'Pompon Rose'.

This derivative of the 'Pompon Rose' came to us from England, where a white variant is also grown in Kennedy's Nursery. Devotees of rose culture have noted over the years an increase in the number of moss roses, often arising from seed of non-mossy ancestors. Bozérian considers that there is a relationship between the branched hairs of a moss rose and the similar appendages of the spongy gall or bedeguar, and that the same insect is responsible for both.

Rosa Pomponiana muscosa.   *Le Pompon mousseux.*

P.J. Redouté pinx.   Imprimerie de Rémond   Victor sculp.

ROSA INDICA FRAGRANS FLORE SIMPLICI
'SINGLE TEA-SCENTED ROSE'

Small *shrub*; *prickles* sparse, straight, dilated at the base. *Leaflets* 3 or 5, elliptic, acute at both ends, glabrous, upperside glossy, margins crenulate; petioles slightly villous, with minute prickles that are more often felt than seen; stipules narrow, denticulate. *Flowers* sweetly scented, 3–4 at the tips of the laterals; peduncles and pedicels glabrous; bracts very narrow, elongated, acute; *receptacles* rounded, glabrous; *sepals* 3 pinnatifid, 2 simple, glabrous, acute, rarely spatulate; *petals* 5, rather large, cordately notched, pale pink; *stamens* long, incurved over the styles as in all China roses. *Heps* subglobose, at first red, black at maturity.

This rose originated as a seedling of the 'Tea-scented Rose' raised at Auteuil in Ternaux's nurseries. It is most notable for the perfume and for the attractive petal colour. It must be kept in a pot and brought into the orangery, as in all tender roses.

Rosa indica fragrans flore simplici.   *Le Bengale the a fleurs simples.*

P. J. Redouté pinx.   Imprimerie de Rémond.   Victor sculp.

ROSA NOISETTIANA PURPUREA
'PINK NOISETTE'

A very beautiful and curious variant of the 'Noisette Rose', but smaller in all its parts. *Shrub* capable of rising to a great height. *Leaflets* darker green when young, less spreading, a little more crumpled. *Flowers* numerous, in fine scented bouquets produced in succession from June up to the frosts; *sepal* appendages setaceous rather than flattened and leafy; *petals* bright pink, deepening as the flower ages, whereas the 'Noisette Rose' begins pale blush and fades to almost white.

Here we have another cultivar that originated in Ternaux's nursery. His head gardener Laffay, who has his own rose nursery, obtained it from seed of the 'Noisette Rose' in 1822. It is thus of hybrid origin, not a species. Its pectinate stipules place it in Group II Floridae of our classification. Both this and the 'Noisette Rose' are now acclimatised in France, having survived the rigours of the winter of 1822 in the open air, and seem destined to ornament our gardens for a long time.

Rosa Noisettiana purpurea,   *Rosier* Noisette a fleurs rouges.

P.J. Redouté hinx.   Imprimerie de Remond   Langlois sculp.

ROSA CANINA BURBONIANA [Thory var. n.]
'BOURBON ROSE'

Tall, vigorous, branched, tufted *shrub; prickles* stout, recurved, dilated, reddish. *Leaflets* 5 or 7, base rounded, apex acute, glabrous on both surfaces, simply dentate, upperside glossy green, underside paler; petioles villous, with small sessile glands and tiny prickles; stipules decurrent, acute, denticulate. *Flowers* sweetly scented, many together at the tips of the laterals; pedicels finely glandular; bracts elongate, ciliate, glandular; *receptacles* ovoid, glabrous; *sepals* pinnatifid with subsetaceous prickles; *petals* 3–4-seriate, cordately notched, brilliant pink. *Heps* rather rounded ovoid, red.

According to the Duke of Orleans, this rose grows in waste places on Reunion Island. Seeds brought from there some years ago produced the plants in the Neuilly gardens from which our painting was made. It has a good habit, and the abundance of blooms, sometimes almost single but mostly semi-double, and their fine colour and perfume make it a worthwhile adornment for landscape gardens.

Rosa Canina Burboniana.   *Rosier de l'Ile de Bourbon.*

P.J. Redouté pinx.   Imprimerie de Rémond.   Langlois sculp.

Στέψον ἇν με και λυρίζω,
Παρὰ σοῖς Διόνυσε, σηκοῖς,
Μετὰ Κόρης βαθυκόλπε,
Ροδίνοισι σεφανίσκοις,
Πεπυκασμενος Χορευσω.

Anacreon Ode V

P. J. Redouté *pinx*   *Imprimerie de Remond*   Charlin *sculp*